LINCOLN CHRISTIAN UNIVER

P9-BVH-113

Leadership Essentials

Practical Tools for Leading in the Church

Carol Cartmill and Yvonne Gentile

Abingdon Press
Nashville

© 2006 by Abingdon Press

All rights reserved. No part of this work may be reproduced or transmitted in any form or by any means, electronic or mechanical, including photocopying and recording, or by any information storage or retrieval system, except as may be expressly permitted by the 1976 Copyright Act or in writing by the publisher. For some material permission to photocopy is granted on the page. Requests for permission should be addressed to Permissions Office, 201 Eighth Avenue, South, P.O. Box 801, Nashville, TN 37202-0801. You may fax your request to 615-749-6128.

Printed in the United States of America.

Scripture quotations in this publication, unless other-wise indicated, are from the *New Revised Standard Version of the Bible*, copyright © 1989 by the Division of Christian Education of the National Council of the Churches of Christ in the United States of America, and are used by permission. All rights reserved.

Those noted NIV are from the HOLY BIBLE, NEW INTERNATIONAL VERSION. Copyright © 1973, 1978, 1984, by International Bible Society. Used by permission of Zondervan Publishing House. All rights reserved.

Those noted KJV are from the King James Version of the Bible.

06 07 08 09 10 11 12 13 14 — 9 8 7 6 5 4 3 2 1

Contents

Introduction

This book arises out of what we perceive is a real need for practical, experiential training in leadership skills for Christian leaders. Churches across the country are searching for leaders to guide and direct the ministries within their congregations. Leaders (existing leaders, new leaders, and even potential leaders) are hungry for tools to equip them to provide excellent leadership. If your church is like most, formalized training for leadership is relatively nonexistent. People find themselves in leadership roles but feel unprepared and ill-equipped to handle the positions. This is not because current church leaders don't want to equip them; they simply do not have the time or resources to do so.

We've experienced this firsthand. At our home congregation, The United Methodist Church of the Resurrection, we offer a leadership development program specifically designed for new and emerging leaders. The program, which utilizes a curriculum we developed entitled *Leadership from the Heart: Learning to Lead with Love and Skill*, provides a spiritual foundation for Christian leadership. At the completion of each program, we ask our participants to assess their needs in terms of further development as leaders—to identify what they need in order to be confident and prepared to lead in the church. The feedback we have received has included comments such as these:

"I need help in the hands-on kinds of things I'm expected to do as a leader. How do I lead a meeting?"

"I have a volunteer who's not showing up for events. How do I confront her without losing her?"

"How do I set the direction for our ministry team? I know where I think we need to go, but I can't seem to get others moving in the same direction. Help!"

"I'm a new leader, and I've never managed a group before. How do I recruit volunteers and then keep them motivated?"

Do any of these responses resonate with you? This book will address the role of leadership from a very practical standpoint. We will provide information on a range of topics, help you understand the importance of each one for you as a Christian leader, and provide tools to assist you in enhancing your skills in these areas. The material is designed to be flexible—either as a resource for individual use or for use in a group training format.

If you use the material for group training, we recommend reading each chapter beforehand, and then working through the activities and the discussion questions during your group time. The material may bring forth questions that relate directly to your situation or your local congregation, and a small group discussion is an ideal forum for gaining insight and ideas from other leaders with similar experiences. We hope this book will become a well-used resource, one you'll keep close by and pull out as needs arise — long after you've read it the first time.

Before we delve into the practical skills, we will first consider the heart of leadership... What kind of leader will you be?

CHAPTER 1

What Kind of Leader Will You Be?

But the Lord said to Samuel, 'DO not look on his appearance or on the height of his stature, because I have rejected him; for the Lord does not see as mortals see; they look on the outward appearance, but the Lord looks on the heart." (1 Samuel 16:7)

I (Yvonne) have experienced the leadership of a number of people over the years: parents and grandparents, aunts and uncles, teachers and pastors, and supervisors and mentors in my career. Some of them were wonderful…and some were not so wonderful. To be fair, I must admit they all had a mix of desirable and undesirable traits. From each one, though, I learned something. I learned the value of gentleness and forgiveness from my mother. One high school teacher challenged me to believe in myself. My favorite aunt taught me that I could disapprove of someone's behavior yet still love the person and treat him or her with respect. Then there were some of the not-so-wonderful lessons. I learned from my hardworking but alcoholic father that harsh words spoken in anger can leave lasting scars, and that I should choose my words carefully. The boss who gave me an opportunity to grow professionally was also a living example of the kind of leadership I did not want to model.

What about the leaders in your life? Think about three leaders or role models you've had over your lifetime. Identify one or two positive traits or skills you have learned from each of them. Which negative traits did they exhibit that you definitely do not want to emulate? Take a moment to record this information here:

Now consider for a moment your own leadership. What values and traits do you desire to model for others? What weaknesses in your leadership skills (it's okay to admit it—we all have them) do you want to overcome, or at least compensate for, so that they don't become the legacy you leave?

Most of us don't spend much time reflecting on this issue, yet doing so can have a lasting impact on our leadership. Have you ever heard the old adage,

"If you don't know where you're going, any road will do"? Or what about this one: "You can't lead people to a place where you are not headed yourself"? Those leaders whose leadership traits or skills we don't admire probably did not set out to be poor leadership examples. More likely, they simply didn't put much thought or intention into how they wanted to lead.

Your leadership will be stronger, and your influence more compelling, if you define ahead of time what kind of leader you will be, and then strive to live into that definition. One way to accomplish this is to develop a values statement. This is different from a mission statement, which defines what you will do. A values statement articulates what you believe, what you value, and how you choose to live. Though you won't live into it perfectly, a values statement helps you chart the course you desire to take and serves as a boundary marker, letting you know when you're off track or warning you before you even begin to head in the wrong direction. It draws a plumb line for your life and leadership.

Leadership in the Character of Christ

Christian leadership isn't something to be taken lightly. It's not about power or prestige, fame or fortune. Entering into a leadership role as a Christian is entering into partnership with God. We become God's agents in the world, guiding and directing the people of God as we work together to complete the mission Christ gave the church when he ascended into heaven: "You will be my witnesses in Jerusalem, in all Judea and Samaria, and to the ends of the earth" (Acts 1:8b).

Make no mistake, if you are a Christian, everything you do witnesses about the authenticity of the gospel to those who are not believers. If you are both a Christian and a leader, your attitudes and actions come under even greater scrutiny. People will watch to see if you live and lead according to the beliefs you profess and Christ is counting on you to do so. We are Christ's physical representation in the world today. We are his spokespersons: "We are ambassadors for Christ, since God is making his appeal through us" (2 Corinthians 5:20a).

Your church is counting on you, too. As a leader—in the church and in the community— you are in a position of influence. It is important that you be a positive influence. This doesn't mean that you won't have questions or disagree with your denomination, your pastor, or other leaders in the congregation. To be a positive influence means you treat those disagreements or questions with respect and discretion, not using them as a platform for public criticism. Though you may disagree on details, as a leader in the church, you need to be able to publicly support the essential work of the pastor, the local body, and the denomination.

When Paul wrote to the Colossians, he said: "Whatever you do, in word or deed, do everything in the name of the Lord Jesus, giving thanks to God the

Father through him" (3:17). Paul's message has dual meaning. In ancient times, a person's name was related to his or her character. Paul is instructing the church not only to be witnesses for Christ, but also to live—in word and deed—with the very character of Christ. In fact, in his Letter to the Ephesians, Paul urges all Christians to "be imitators of God, as beloved children, and live in love, as Christ loved us and gave himself up for us" (5:1).

As Christian leaders, being intentional about leading in the name of Christ, in the very character of Christ, is crucial. We can't afford just to "wing it" and hope our leadership honors God almost accidentally. We must decide what kind of leader we will be, put it in writing, and make living it a daily commitment.

Beyond Leadership Styles

You've probably read a number of books on leadership. Each one has its own list of leadership styles: transactional, transformational, authoritative, autocratic, democratic, participative, and so forth. Each of these styles has its own strengths and weaknesses. The best leaders use a combination of styles, depending on the situation and people they are leading.

What we are talking about goes beyond leadership styles to your heart as a leader. Who are you as a person? What fundamental beliefs lie beneath your behavior and your decision processes? What values do you hold as most important to your life? All these factors will play a role in determining your primary leadership style, but they are more far-reaching than your role as a leader; they will impact every facet of your life.

A value is a belief or standard a person regards as integral to how he or she lives. Some of our values may have been with us forever (though perhaps we weren't aware of that fact), while some may rise out of our life experiences. Our values may change, or at least change in priority, over the course of our life. A single value can encompass all areas of life or primarily relate to one segment of life, such as business or family, though it may still impact every area of your life. For instance, if one of your values is integrity, you are going to struggle if you are asked by your boss to skirt the edge of ethics to make a sale. Likewise, you won't be comfortable telling your spouse a little white lie about how much money you spent. If family time is one of your primary values, it may relate primarily to your personal life. But it also will influence your decisions about how much time you commit to leisure pursuits with your friends as well as professional activities outside of normal business hours. Taken together, your values weave a tapestry of who you are at heart.

Developing Your Values Statement

So what are your values? Sometimes it's easier to start with a list and use it to either confirm what you already know or to begin a process of elimination. Below is a list of common values. It is not a complete list, so let it simply spark your creativity. Feel free to add a value that may not be on the list. Circle or make a mark by the five values that seem to appeal most to you:

Accomplishment	Goodness	Problem solving
Accountability	Good will	Progress
Accuracy	Gratitude	Prosperity
Adventure	Hard work	Punctuality
Beauty	Harmony	Quality of work
Challenge	Health	Resourcefulness
Change	Honesty	Respect for others
Collaboration	Honor	Responsiveness
Commitment	Independence	Results-oriented
Communication	Influence	Safety
Community	Inner peace	Satisfying others
Competence	Innovation	Security
Concern for others	Integrity	Self-expression
Continuous improvement	Joy	Self-sacrifice
Cooperation	Justice	Self-reliance
Creativity	Knowledge	Service
Decisiveness	Leadership	Significance
Democracy	Love	Simplicity
Discipline	Loyalty	Skill
Discovery	Money	Stability
Education	Openness	Status
Efficiency	Organization	Strength
Equality	Peace	Teamwork
Excellence	Personal growth	Timeliness
Fairness	Physical work	Tolerance
Faith	Pleasure	Tradition
Family	Positive attitude	Tranquility
Freedom	Power	Trust
Friendship	Practicality	Truth
Fun Preservation	Privacy	Unity
Global view		Variety

It's important to recognize that these values are neither good nor evil on their own. It's how we define what each one means to us and how we prioritize them that really matters. I may value prosperity because I want to be rich and have the ability to buy all the "finer things in life" for my own pleasure. You may value prosperity because you want to be able to leave a financial legacy for your family, or fund a charitable foundation, or donate money to your church's missions projects. Our next step is to work on putting your values statement together. Keep in mind that it is helpful to revisit your values statement on a regular basis. As you strive to live into it with intentionality, you may want to revise it, reword it, or rearrange it. The following format is just an example. If you feel creative, let those juices flow! Just make sure you have enough detail in your values statement to make it clear and meaningful.

To get you started, here's my (Yvonne's) values statement:

I Believe:

That God is the Creator of all things; and that his Son, Jesus Christ, died on the cross and, on the third day, rose from the grave for the forgiveness of my sin;
That God created me for a purpose and has called me to use my gifts of teaching, administration, and leadership in service to the Body of Christ and to the world.

To find happiness, fulfillment, and meaning in life, I will live according to the following values:

Integrity

I will be a person others find trustworthy. I will speak only those things useful for building others up, and I will keep my word. I will strive to live my life as an example of Christ's love to others.

Humility

Though my life has not always been easy, I have been blessed with many gifts and abilities. I have achieved much in life through hard work and the grace of God. I will always remember where I came from, and I will not think more highly of myself than others.

Service

I often find myself in a position of leadership. I will strive to be a leader after the example of Christ — in other words, a servant-leader. I will expend my energy trying to help those I lead to grow personally and achieve their goals.

Respect

I will remember that every person I meet is a child of God, and I will treat them with respect, even when we disagree.

Education

I have a true love of learning, and I commit to being a student throughout my life, whether formally or informally. I will use my spiritual gifts of teaching, administration, and leadership to share what I learn to benefit others and to glorify God.

Making It Personal

First, think about the fundamental beliefs that drive or influence everything you do. What are they? Try to keep this section to two or three points:

Now, what are the key values you identified as important to you? List each one, giving a short definition that explains what it means to you. Remember, there are no right or wrong answers here. Each person may approach the same value from a different perspective. These are your personal values, and the definitions will be as unique as you are!

Once you've completed this exercise, you may want to write or type your values statement in a more formal format and keep it somewhere easily accessible so that you can review it regularly.

Questions for Reflection or Discussion

1. If you're in a group study, discuss some of the lessons you've learned from various leaders in your life – both good and bad. How have those lessons influenced your own leadership?

2. What does it mean to lead "in the name (character) of Christ"? What impact will striving to live into that concept have on your leadership?

3. How hard was it to identify and define your values? Why do you think it's important to do so?

4. What difference do you think having a values statement will make in your leadership and your life?

CHAPTER 2

Making Disciples

Remember your leaders, those who spoke the word of God to you; consider the outcome of their way of life, and imitate their faith. (Hebrews 13:7)

In chapter 1, we considered who we desire to be as leaders. This is a solid foundation from which to start. Maybe you are familiar with the saying, "We teach what we know, but we reproduce who we are." That is a sobering thought, but with God's grace, we're up for the challenge.

Now we turn our attention to our role in developing others. Here, we will evoke another familiar statement: "Begin with the end in mind." Before you begin the process of developing people for leadership, you must have a clear vision of the leader that, with God's help, you aspire to produce.

Beginning with the end in mind, take a few moments to think about leadership in your church. Jot down a list of the character traits, behaviors, and attributes you believe are important for a church leader:

Now review your list. Place a check mark next to the words or phrases on your list that also are descriptive of a disciple—someone who is earnestly seeking to follow after the example of Jesus' life and teachings.

If you were making a list to describe only a disciple, what would you add?

As you review the second list, do you see anything that is not also important for a leader? Our hope is that what you have created with these two lists is the beginning of a vision of the kind of leaders you hope to produce in your church.

Discipleship Is Integral to Leadership Development

We recognize Matthew 28:19-20 as The Great Commission. We might argue these are the marching orders for our churches:

Go therefore and make disciples of all nations, baptizing them in the name of the Father and of the Son and of the Holy Spirit, and teaching them to obey everything I have commanded you. And remember, I am with you always, to the end of the age.

Let's focus on one aspect of this commission, "make disciples." Churches are called to make disciples. Not all of our discipleship programs and ministries are meant to produce church leaders, but all of our church leaders need to be, first and foremost, disciples.

Why is this so important? Let me (Carol) share from personal experience...and pain. I have witnessed firsthand the damage that can be done when church leaders are not following in the footsteps of Christ. I have observed the impact to ministries and to people. Ministries led by such leaders have quickly lost mission focus or have ceased to function in harmony with the rest of the church. People serving under such leaders, or being served by the ministries led by such leaders, have been wounded when they no longer experienced Christ-like love, mercy, and grace. Paul speaks to this in his first letter to the church at Corinth when he writes:

If I speak in the tongues of mortals and of angels, but do not have love, I am a noisy gong or a clanging symbol. And if I have prophetic powers, and understand all mysteries and all knowledge, and if I have all faith, so as to remove mountains, but do not have love, I am nothing. (1 Corinthians 13:1-2)

Leadership without the proper care and consideration of others, which are the marks of a disciple of Christ, is empty. Remember, in addition to living into the Great Commission, we are also called to follow the Great Commandment:

You shall love the Lord your God with all your heart, and with all your soul, and with all your mind, and with all your strength...you shall love your neighbor as yourself. (Mark 12:30-31a)

Leadership skills are essential, but we are first called to be instruments of God who are guiding others toward spiritual growth and maturity. Not all disciples will be called into leadership roles, but let's be sure those who are leaders are grounded in the faith, building their leadership and ministry on the foundation of a growing relationship with God. In this way, we can better ensure the effectiveness of ministry, the self-care and development of the leader, and the care of those influenced by the leader.

Let's be clear—it is the work of the Holy Spirit to affect the kind of life transformation necessary to make disciples of people. What we as church leaders are about is creating the right culture or environment in which the Holy Spirit will work.

Disciple-making is likely a key component of your church's purpose statement. Let me share with you a sample purpose statement of a church that is committed to making disciples, along with its definitions of both a "disciple of Christ" and "discipleship."

> **Purpose Statement:** The purpose of our church is to reach out to non-religious and nominally religious people, bringing them into a Christian community where they can grow in relationship and faith with God and others as disciples of Christ.

> **A disciple of Christ is**…someone who seeks to follow the teachings of Jesus and the life he modeled for us through a deepening knowledge of God and the Bible (we know God with our head), a growing personal relationship with God and others (we love God with our heart), and a life of faith that is evident to those around us (we serve God and others with our hands).

> **Discipleship is**…the lifelong process of growing in Christ-likeness as we seek to know God, love God, and serve God in community and out in the world.

> **Leadership is discipleship**…kicked up a notch. It is discipleship that has progressed to the point where the disciple is spiritually prepared and equipped to guide others along in the journey we know as the Christian life. Leadership is influencing others for the cause of Christ.

Discipleship needs to be an integral component of leadership development. Let's talk about how to make this vision a reality.

1. Be Intentional About Planning for Transformation

A number of years ago, I (Carol) was serving in a church that was experiencing a bit of turmoil amongst some of its long-term leaders. These leaders seemed to be out of step with the mission and vision of the church to the point where they started creating dissension in committee meetings and the Bible study classes they were leading. It seemed out-of-character for individuals who were considered "pillars of the church" to suddenly become vocal critics of the direction the church was taking on certain issues.

Several of these leaders eventually left the church and our senior staff was left wondering, *What just happened?* It was only in retrospect that the realization hit: We had not been paying close attention to our discipleship process. Specifically, while we offered a lot of great Bible study classes and discipleship programs, we were not intentional enough about asking ourselves what we hoped to produce through those classes. Our discipleship ministries were not consistently producing disciples.

We discovered a gap between offering biblical knowledge and "making disciples." The outcome? There were people who had amassed a great deal of head knowledge, but it was not leading to life change. People were taking classes and learning a great deal about the Bible, but they had no idea how to translate information into transformation. Again, this is ultimately the work of the Holy Spirit, but we found we could do a much better job of creating an environment where transformation might actually happen.

Of course, this example is a generalization. While we may have been caught off guard by the outcome for the aforementioned leaders, many people in our classes were growing and maturing

Envision what you hope the participant in the class will know or be able to do at the end of the class.

spiritually. There was, however, a common denominator among the more successful classes and programs. The leaders of those ministries were not just teachers or facilitators; they were being used by God as "disciple-makers." The leaders clearly communicated a preferred outcome for their ministries and intentionally planned in order to achieve that outcome. They engaged, supported, encouraged, and challenged participants to live into what was being taught.

What does it mean to be intentional about planning for transformation — about making disciples? First, identify the objective of the ministry or class you are offering. Envision what you hope the participant in the class will know or be able to do at the end of the class. Perhaps you are teaching a class on evangelism. If so, your objective might be something like this:

> Participants in the evangelism class will have a biblical understanding of the need and plan for salvation, a personal assurance of their own salvation, the ability to articulate their own personal faith story, and a concrete plan for sharing that story with others.

Now you have a target toward which you can aim. Having this target will help you as you choose curriculum, outline the teaching sessions, market the class, and evaluate your results.

We also need to set some expectations, both for ourselves as ministry leaders and for our participants. Using this same example, what expectations might we set for our evangelism ministry? What can the participants in the class reasonably expect as a result of investing their time, and perhaps money, in taking the class? We might say:

> We will provide teaching and resources on the biblical basis
> for salvation. Leaders will be available to meet one-on-one
> with participants who have personal faith questions.
> Participants will have the opportunity to consider and write
> their personal faith story, share that story in the safety of the
> classroom, and create an action plan for sharing their faith
> with others.

Along with setting expectations on the church's side, you will want to set expectations for your class members. These might include consistent attendance, homework completion, active participation in the class or group, and respect for other members of the class. If these expectations cannot be met, it is better for a participant to take the class at a later time when they can.

Once you have set goals for the ministry or class and expectations for the leaders and participants, you need a plan of communication. Take a look at your marketing materials. If you create some form of brochure or flyer, be sure it accurately describes the ministry. Expectations also should be shared in the orientation or introductory session of any class, study, or program offered by the church.

You also will need a plan for receiving feedback from the participants at the end of the class or course so that you will know whether or not you achieved the desired results. Written evaluations are helpful here, especially if they can be completed anonymously. Keep the form simple—no more than one page—and ask open-ended questions such as these:

◆ As you reflect on your classroom experiences, describe how the program successfully met your expectations.

◆ What would have improved your level of satisfaction?

◆ What did you enjoy most about the class?

◆ On a scale of 1 (low) to 5 (high), how effective was this class in equipping you to… (for example, articulate and share your faith)? Please describe.

Additional comments or suggestions:

The exercise of writing a vision and mission statement is vitally important as well. Having clearly stated objectives, which are realized through planning and execution and are evaluated through a formal feedback process at the end of the class, makes all the difference in the world.

We're going to give you an opportunity to apply this type of intentionality to one of your existing programs at the end of the chapter. Once you develop this skill, you can bring the same level of planning to all of your teaching ministries. Soon you will be maximizing your effectiveness in partnership with the Holy Spirit to produce committed disciples.

2. Incorporate Reflection Into Ministry/Service Experiences

Another way we can be intentional in our efforts to include discipleship in the development of our leaders is to build times of reflection into ministry service. At least in our church, activity comes very naturally—we are by nature "doers." Once we have accomplished a task or service project, we rush on to the next one. This leaves little or no room to reflect upon how God was at work through us as we used our gifts in service, what results God achieved through our efforts, or how our service contributed to the mission and vision of our church.

It's very simple to incorporate reflection into our service experiences, and it's a wonder we do not do so more often. While you can create formal reflection tools, I (Carol) have found it effective to take time immediately after an event or a project's completion to gather the team around for a time of debriefing and prayer.

We gather informally at a table, or we stand or sit in a circle. Then we start with some thought-provoking questions, such as:

◆ What went right today?
◆ How and where did you sense God at work?
◆ Specifically, how did God use you? What impact does that have on your faith?
◆ How did this service impact the mission/vision of our church?
◆ What is our next step?

Finally, we spend time in prayer, thanking God for what has happened and for allowing our team members to be a part of the work of God's ministry.

Building reflection into ministry on a regular basis not only will bring meaning to the tasks you are about; it also will have an impact on the spiritual growth of the individual members of the service team. People will make connections between their faith and their service for God. Just as Jesus served others (see Luke 19:10), so also his disciples are called to do likewise.

3. Embrace Head, Heart and Hands Discipleship

Earlier in the chapter we suggested that a disciple of Christ is someone who seeks to follow the teachings of Jesus and the life he modeled for us through a deepening knowledge of God and the Bible (we know God with our *head*), a growing personal relationship with God and others (we love God with our *heart*), and a life of faith that is evident to those around us (we serve God and others with our *hands*).

The church we attend believes that in order for our programs to grow disciples, participants need to experience God with their heads, with their hearts, and through their hands. So often in our planning, churches tend to focus on the logistics of the particular ministries and programs, not the outcomes. They communicate a simple message in marketing these, which is simply "take this class." People sometimes find themselves involved in programs without a clear understanding of "why" and have no idea where the program is leading. We must remember that our programs and ministries are the tools, the vehicles, for helping us become disciples. They are not the destination. In our church, we try to offer a clear picture of the outcomes and we attempt to incorporate elements of all three components—head, heart and hands—into each and every ministry of the church.

> # Spiritual leaders not only equip their followers; they care for them in thought, word, and deed.

Building in a "head" component means we take time to reference Scripture as it relates to what we are hoping to accomplish through our ministry. This can be done through a short devotion or a more in-depth study of the Bible. Learning to know God with our heads involves taking in information through reading, hearing, and reflecting on Scripture and theological teachings. We grow to become more theologically informed Christians.

Growing to love God with our hearts involves considering how what we have learned with our heads can be applied to our lives and our relationships. Attending to the "heart" can be done in several ways. We generally use prayer, worship, reflection, small group interaction (a community element), or some combination of the four to bring us closer to the heart of God and closer to one another.

Finally, because we recognize that disciples live out their faith in tangible ways, a "hands" element is built into all we do. This involves developing an action plan to implement the concepts of the faith we are learning into our everyday lives. We learn to do the things Jesus did—or would do now. Bible study and home-based small groups take time to participate in service projects together, usually serving in mission outside the walls of the church. Even our leadership development groups engage in mission projects and are challenged to set an evangelism goal, such as inviting someone without a church home to join them in worship.

Various programs within the church may have a stronger focus in one of the three areas—head, hands, or heart. For example, our mission and service ministries spend most of their time concentrating on "hands" discipleship, but they do not neglect the head and heart. Our in-depth Bible studies, which are curricula-driven, have an emphasis on gaining head knowledge about God, but they also include elements of heart and hands. Our home-based small groups are very relational and tend to have a heart focus, but they are intentional in incorporating head and hands activities into the life of their communities. Don't think about this approach in the context of a pie you would split into three equal pieces but rather as approaches to discipleship you hold in tension. Including all three dimensions, however, will increase the likelihood that transformation will occur.

Think about the ministry programming of your church. If you are intentional about planning for transformation, helping people to relate what they are experiencing in ministry to their spiritual lives, and striving for balance through head, heart, and hands discipleship, you will have done much to create an environment for disciple-making to be realized.

A Spiritual Foundation for Leadership

To this point, we have been focused on how to build our leadership on the foundation of effective discipleship, which is spiritual in nature. It's critical to have a spiritual foundation for leadership, and one is built first upon our own relationship with God. Effective leaders are continually growing in their personal faith relationship through cultivating spiritual disciplines in their lives such as prayer, Bible study, worship, and service. This translates to leadership in the power of the Holy Spirit and the ability to model Christian character to those who follow.

A spiritual foundation includes having a mission and vision for ministry that is in alignment with the mission and vision of the church. Our top leadership cannot actively oversee every ministry happening throughout the church. What happens when leaders are leading people in a direction counter to the church's vision? The outcome is not generally good. As we build discipleship into leadership development, we must be intentional in teaching to the mission and vision of the church.

Finally, as we provide a spiritual foundation for leadership, we must teach about our responsibilities toward those we lead. Spiritual leaders not only equip their followers; they care for them in thought, word, and deed. They model servant leadership as they find opportunities to serve those they lead.

We choose to build our leadership development efforts on a spiritual foundation of solid discipleship, because leadership in the church is as much a work of our hearts as it is a skill we develop. People are more important than processes. They are what ministry is all about. We can create efficient programs and train leaders to be technically proficient, but "what will it profit

them if they gain the whole world but forfeit their life?"(Matthew 16:26)
At the end of the day, when our leaders have finished their service, it is our desire for them to have experienced the presence of Christ in that service and in their personal lives. The fruit of this approach is more effective ministry.

In summary, making disciples is the first step toward developing leaders. Not all followers of Christ become leaders, but all leaders are first disciples. As churches, we, with the guidance of the Holy Spirit, create more effective environments for the process of discipleship as we

- ◆ become more intentional in our planning of programs and classes
- ◆ offer tools for post-service reflection
- ◆ incorporate head, heart, and hands activities for holistic discipleship
- ◆ build our leadership development on a spiritual foundation

Beginning with the next chapter, we will shift our focus to developing leadership skills, delving into tasks and processes that, once mastered, will result in more effective ministry.

Questions for Reflection or Discussion

1. Use the worksheet in the Appendix (p. 117) to evaluate one of your existing classes or programs. Discuss what you learned in completing this exercise.

2. Reflect on the impact serving has had on your own personal spiritual development. In what ways does serving Christ and others help you grow spiritually?

3. List some of the options in your church for people to deepen their knowledge of God and the Bible (know God with their head), grow in personal relationship with God and others (love God with their heart), and live their faith in the world (serve God with their hands). Why are all three important? How might you encourage your members to become more balanced between the three components?

4. Describe the points in your own life where spiritual growth intersects with your leadership. How are you, personally, growing in head, heart, and hands faith?

CHAPTER 3

Building and Sustaining Teams

And he said to them, "Follow me, and I will make you fish for people."
(Matthew 4:19)

Building and sustaining quality ministry teams is perhaps the most important skill a leader can develop, for the scope and effectiveness of ministry can be multiplied exponentially through a team. As ministry leaders, we cannot afford to go it alone—it is too costly for us individually and for the ministries we represent.

Jesus modeled how to build a ministry team when he called and mentored the disciples. He invested in the twelve in a way that would make possible the continuation of his ministry on earth after his ascension into heaven. When I (Carol) have become discouraged by the challenges of team-building, it encourages me to know that even Jesus experienced some of the same pitfalls of leadership (one team member in particular did not pan out). Yet his investment paid off in the long run, and so can ours.

Building a great team takes time and intentionality. The processes of inviting people to the team, equipping and resourcing them to serve, and caring for and sustaining them once they are active in ministry are ongoing. While engaged in activities and tasks, teams are relationship-driven, and, as such, they demand regular attention.

One of the best and most succinct definitions of *team* I have run across comes from *The Equipping Church Guidebook*, co-authored by Sue Mallory and Brad Smith:

> A team is a group of people with complimentary and
> diverse skills, spiritual gifts, and strengths who are
> committed to
>> Sharing a common purpose
>> Loving and supporting each other
>> Achieving the team's mission
>> Holding each other accountable
> (Grand Rapids, MI: Zondervan, 2001, p. 69)

Teams are not collections of like-minded individuals, for there are often differing opinions among team members. Healthy conflict is actually good for the team and the work of ministry. The "glue" that holds the team together is relational trust and unity of purpose. In this chapter, we will explore how to build and sustain healthy ministry teams.

Before we go on, I'd like to say a quick word about what might be a more familiar organizational structure to many in the church: the committee. Although committees and teams are both groups of people accomplishing church work, they serve different purposes.

Committees generally are led by a chairperson, function according to by-laws, are more formal in nature, and are formed through a process of nominations and elections. They best perform the maintenance, governance, policy-making, and oversight functions on behalf of the church. Churches need committees to handle matters of finance, administration, buildings, and staffing. Churches benefit from investing in these bodies as a whole, as well as in the individuals who comprise them.

Teams have leaders, too, but the team leader is likely someone who has emerged as a recognized "talent" with the passion for the specific ministry for which the team is responsible. Team members are invited rather than elected. While committees make ministry possible, often providing resources such as money and staff, teams are more "hands on" in nature, mobilizing people to carry out ministry.

If your church functions with committees only, it might be helpful to evaluate if there are functions that would be better managed through a team. Many churches utilize teams for their missions, children's, youth, women's, men's, adult discipleship, singles, and other service-related ministries. If the ministry group can operate creatively, is not required to follow written policies and procedures, and can make decisions collaboratively rather than by formal voting procedures, then the team structure may be the optimal choice. Keep in mind, however, that the concepts shared in this chapter apply to both teams and committees as long as your goals are to create more effective ministry and a deepening sense of community among group members.

Reflecting on Your Team Experiences

At one time or another, most everyone has been a part of a team through involvement in sports, school, work, or church. Our experiences tend to shape our views toward teams, either positively or negatively. We can learn from both. Positive experiences can serve as a starting point for developing effective team-building skills, and negative experiences can help us avoid certain behaviors we do not find productive. The following questions are meant to help you reflect on your experiences. Think of a team in which you were significantly involved and answer the following:

◆ What was the name of the team, and what was the team's purpose? Was that purpose made clear?
◆ How effective was the team leader? Describe what made him or her effective or ineffective.
◆ How many team members were there, and what were their individual roles? Describe the various contributions made by each team member.

- Explain how team members were invited to join the team, equipped to serve in their various roles, and cared for while a part of the team.
- How effective was the team in achieving its purpose? Why was it successful or unsuccessful?
- If you could turn back the clock, what would you do to enhance the team's effectiveness?

Creating and Sustaining a Team

One great dynamic of teams is synergy. Synergy is the interaction of two or more forces creating a combined effect that is greater than the sum of their individual effects. Cooperative interaction in teams creates an enhanced, combined effect and produces a greater outcome. Have you ever been in a room where the creative juices of people are flowing freely? Do you get jazzed just thinking about the possibilities of such an amazing team? Do you believe it's possible for you to build a synergistic team? It definitely is! In Luke 10, we find the account of the mission of the seventy. Jesus appointed seventy individuals for ministry and sent them out in pairs. In verse 17 we read, "The seventy returned with joy, saying, 'Lord, in your name even the demons submit to us!'" The seventy had been as successful in their mission as Jesus would have been if he had gone out on his own—even more so when you consider their numbers. They were given a clear purpose and explicit instructions, they were sent out in the power of God, and they traveled in pairs. At the end of the mission, they were able to rejoice in the mission's success with one another and with their leader. Luke 10 provides us with the inspiration to involve others in ministry, a model for equipping others to serve, and a reminder to celebrate once the mission has been accomplished.

Serving alone can be challenging, not to mention lonely.

A team environment is also optimal in terms of the support it provides for the individual member. Serving alone can be challenging, not to mention lonely. Healthy teams provide members with encouragement, a sense of community, and a measure of accountability. Members share the workload. Teams enhance existing programs, generate fresh ideas for new endeavors, and serve as effective forums for problem-solving. This takes the pressure off, keeping one person from being expected to have all the answers and do all the work. Learning to create and sustain teams is worth the effort.

So, where do you start? Let's start by taking a look at five common denominators in successful teams.

1. The Team Has a Clear Vision and Mission

Being lost or adrift can create feelings of anxiety. There's something about having a clear sense of direction that inspires confidence. Effective teams know clearly why they exist and whom they are called to serve. There's also a sense among the team that all members, even though they might be playing different positions, are moving the ball in the same direction—aiming toward the same goal. A clearly articulated mission also helps the team to evaluate its effectiveness at the end of the game.

In the Chapter 5 we'll define in greater detail the processes for creating vision and mission statements as well as describe how they differ. Generally, a team should create its own mission statement, and the team mission statement should tie back to the vision and mission statements of the church. For example, if the church's vision statement is "transforming the community and individual lives," the team should be able to point to something specific about its work that supports life or community transformation. So, the vision and mission statement of a mission-related team that serves an inner-city homeless shelter might identify how its work contributes to community transformation.

In a nutshell, a mission statement should help your team to

◆ understand what the team is supposed to do and why—and what it should *not* do
◆ appreciate the importance of the team's role within the community or church
◆ evaluate challenges and celebrate successes
◆ communicate the work of the team to others outside the team
◆ focus its creativity, efforts, energy, and thinking

A worksheet for creating a mission statement is included in the Appendix (p. 120). Take the time to work through this process with your team, and revisit your mission every time you add a new team member.

2. Members Reflect Diversity With Unity

First Corinthians 12 speaks to the topic of spiritual gifts. A recurring theme within this passage is "one body with many members." This applies to healthy teams. Any given team will be made up of several different individuals—many members, one team. In verses 4-6 we read, "Now there are varieties of gifts, but the same Spirit; and there are varieties of services, but the same Lord; and there are varieties of activities, but it is the same God who activates all of them in everyone." Different...but the same.

Paul's use of the analogy of the human body in 1 Corinthians 12 helps us to understand why this diversity is by God's design. How useful would a body be if it were made up solely of eyes or ears or hands? Each part is important; each plays its role in the overall functioning of the body. The fact that these roles are different is critical to the body's effectiveness.

Effective teams have a diversity of gifting and styles. A team would not be very balanced if it were comprised only of administrators. The detail work would get done, but who would provide the vision or creativity? If the team included only big-picture-thinking extroverts who can cast vision and market ideas, who would pay attention to the deadlines and budgets of the project at hand?

It's somewhat natural to want to surround ourselves with people who act and think like we do, but give some thought to the last time you were a part of creating something special. Did anyone along the way help to shape a better outcome by challenging your initial thinking? It takes all kinds of people to make this world go 'round!

When you build your team, make sure you include people who will serve as big-picture vision casters, people-engaging cheerleaders, detail-focused administrators, and task-focused implementers. Recruit people who are unified around the mission of the team and are passionate about the ministry but who also express their loyalty to the team according to their individual styles and gifts. As with our human body parts, each individual, though a part of the whole, will have his or her own role to play.

3. Team Members Share Responsibilities and Bear Burdens Together

The individuals on an effective team take ownership of the team mission and actively participate according to their spiritual gifts, talents, and styles. In 1 Corinthians 12:26, Paul writes, "If one member suffers, all suffer together with it; if one member is honored, all rejoice together with it." Team members have a sense that "we're all in this together."

A baseball team sends nine players out on the field when the opposing team is at bat. How successful would the team be if only the pitcher and catcher decided to contribute? If they were exceptionally gifted and very fast, the two might be able to cover a portion of the infield if the batter made contact with the ball; but what would happen if the ball were hit to the left field warning track?

Every member of the team must be "in the game," operating within the framework of a well-defined role. Of course, there will be times when a team member may need to step away for a season, perhaps due to a personal or family crisis. When this happens, team members surround this person with love and care and are willing to shoulder additional responsibilities until that member can rejoin their efforts. And when he or she returns, there is great rejoicing!

The team leader facilitates the sharing of the workload, which involves creating descriptions for the various roles on the team. It is important for each person to have a clear understanding of his or her assignment between meetings. It's great if team members can pair off to work on assignments, but this is not always feasible or efficient. As the team works together, people figure out their strengths and weaknesses and learn how to cooperate and collaborate on their efforts.

The team leader can also model sharing responsibilities by assigning various team members leadership over different portions of the next scheduled meeting. For example, if you include a short devotion in your meetings, ask another team member to prepare it. Prepare a sign-up sheet with the dates of the next few meetings, and ask team members to sign up to bring treats. Ask another member to lead prayer, follow up with absentees, or plan a group service project. Before you do anything, ask yourself, "Is this something I could ask someone else to do?" If the answer is "yes," then go ahead and ask.

4. There Is a Foundation of Trust Built on Healthy Relationships

In order to build and sustain an effective team, the team must have a solid foundation of trust; and in order to build and sustain trust, you must work toward developing strong relationships. The work of developing relationships takes time and intentional effort. There are no shortcuts. In fact, you often will pay an initial price of lost productivity—at least in the short run.

If you have a brand new team, you will need to start with simple introductions and connecting activities. Every meeting should include a warm up designed to help individuals reveal something personal about themselves (for example, life outside of the team, family, hobbies, interests). The goal is to move people toward a place where they will feel comfortable being vulnerable with one another as you create Christian community.

Another way to create a sense of community is to end every meeting by sharing personal prayer concerns. We often play it safe, bringing up our concerns for church or family members—even neighbors or coworkers. Model "getting real" by sharing something personal for which you would enjoy the benefit of others' prayers. At the following meeting, be sure to let the team know the outcome so that they can either celebrate with you or continue to persevere in prayer on your behalf.

Relationships are strengthened when team members have the opportunity to fellowship outside of the context of a regularly scheduled meeting. Some teams plan a social event in which other family members or special friends can also be included. It's said that food brings people together, so plan a simple meal or cookout. Perhaps the team might plan a mission service project together—something that is outside the scope of their normal tasks. Working together to serve the needs of others naturally brings people closer—especially if time is taken afterward to reflect together on the service experience.

Engage in a group activity that encourages spiritual growth. This might take the form of a devotion, a regular time of prayer, worship and communion, or a spiritual retreat. Attend a conference together or encourage all members to read a particular book relating to the work of the team. Learning together is an awesome tool for team bonding.

Finally, create a team covenant together, and revisit it annually or as new people join the team. A template is included in the Appendix (p. 123). The covenant lays out the vision, values, expectations, and behaviors of the team. Agreeing to these elements up front will help the team to avoid conflict and frustration down the road. For example, if a team member starts to grumble about the number of times the team is meeting, you could revisit the place in the covenant that speaks of the agreed upon meeting frequency, and so on.

5. The Team Observes Three Sustaining Practices: Reflection, Evaluation, and Celebration

We live life at a fast pace. This also can be true of our ministry teams. We plan for one event and, as soon as the event has ended, immediately start planning the next without pausing for reflection, evaluation, or celebration. These three actions are important in terms of long-term ministry effectiveness and team development.

Reflection is intentionally taking time to recount the details and impact of an event. Perhaps the team spent six months planning a Vacation Bible School (VBS) for neighborhood children and one week actually holding the event. Why not take an hour to gather the VBS staff together for an informal time of sharing stories? You can seed

> **Learning together is an awesome tool for team bonding.**

these by asking every team member to answer simple questions such as "What was the highlight of the week for you?"; "Where did you see God at work?"; and "We were here to teach the children, but what did you learn?" Sharing the answers to such questions will cement the event in people's memories as well as bring the team closer together.

Evaluation is also a useful and necessary tool. By nature, we humans generally like to know how well we do at the tasks we perform. Most of us also welcome criticism when it is constructive and it helps us to do better in the future. We want to succeed. The same holds true for teams. It benefits the team to evaluate the work that it does and its effectiveness in light of its stated mission.

Evaluations can be done formally in a written or web-based format, or informally as a topic of open discussion during a meeting. You should have three goals in mind when conducting any evaluation: (1) to identify what is being done well—specifically, what has been successful that you might want to repeat, (2) to target areas for improvement—what you might do differently next time, or not at all, and (3) to generate ideas for doing something new—seeds for creating a new ministry or event.

Finally, take time to celebrate the team's accomplishments. Think about simple and inexpensive gifts you can make or purchase for team members that have a direct tie to the ministry. For example, a women's ministry team known as P.I.E. (pursue—imagine—empower) held an event where every woman on the team was given an actual pie, as in apple, cherry, and banana cream. A staff member responsible for small groups purchased a leadership book by a well-known Christian author as gifts for members of her coaching team. Some leaders invite team members to their homes for a potluck cookout, while others have them gather at a restaurant. The key is to be sure to name what is being celebrated and to reinforce the truth that it took the contributions of many team members to realize the dream.

Three Steps to Building a Team

By now, you have a clear mental picture of an effective ministry team. Now let us shift the focus from the dynamics of the team to actually building one. Again, this will take time and intentional effort. Learning three basic steps will help you to build an amazing ministry team.

1. Extend an Invitation

Some churches have established a rule that a new ministry cannot launch unless there are at least four people committed to serve on the supporting team for that ministry. Perhaps you are inviting people to join a brand new team. If this is the case, you will have less in terms of a clearly defined role to offer, but some will view being invited to a new venture as an exciting opportunity to get in on the ground floor and help shape the ministry. If you are recruiting for openings on an existing team, you will be able to share more specific details about the work of the team and the individual role of the team member.

Here are a few ideas to keep in mind in either case:

◆ *Be prepared to articulate the mission and vision of the team.* For an existing team, the mission and vision may be well defined. In the case of a new ministry, you will at least have a defined ministry direction even if the details are sketchy. For example, if you are starting an audio-video support ministry at the church, you can share where A/V support will be used in the church and how the work of the team will support the church's overall mission and objectives. Articulating the purpose of the team will help in the individual's decision-making process. If the team vision and mission spark an interest or ignite a passion, chances are you have found a potential team member.

◆ *Define the individual role or roles within the team.* What are you asking the recruit to consider doing as a team member? You may have something very specific in mind—"We need someone to handle marketing and communications on behalf of the team. You would need to write publicity pieces and develop and implement creative marketing strategies for our ministry." You also will need to realistically state the time commitment. Think in terms of the number of hours per week or month it will take to accomplish the tasks of the position. Include in this figure information about meetings the team member is expected to attend. You may find the Ministry Position Description in the Appendix (p. 138) to be a useful tool in this process.

◆ *Give advance thought and prayer to the person you will ask.* Think about whom you already know with the right mix of gifts and passion to fill the role. Network with other leaders in the church to develop a list of potential candidates. Ask God to give you the eyes to see the people you should consider. In addition to gifts and passions, you also need to consider the availability of the potential team member. The people we ask need to be able to carve enough space out of life to devote to the work of the team. Every team member must pull his or her own weight and contribute. Finally, consider the individual's previous church-related experience. Does his or her prior involvement demonstrate the right heart, aptitude, and commitment to be considered for a role on your team?

> **If the team vision and mission spark an interest or ignite a passion, chances are you have found a potential team member.**

◆ *Do the "ask."* Once you have sketched out the team member's role and identified a person to invite, you need to actually ask him or her to join the team. Choose a time and setting that lends itself to having a meaningful conversation—one that is quiet and unhurried. Be prepared to give the individual you are asking information about the team and the position on the team in writing. Tell the individual exactly why you believe he or she is a good candidate. Invite the candidate to pray with you about joining the team. If the role is on an existing team, share the name or names of others on the team with whom this person might also visit about the opportunity. Have a predetermined time to talk about a final decision—usually one week is ample time—and be sure you are available to answer questions that might be raised during the decision-making process. Finally, ask with confidence. Most people are very receptive to a personal invitation that has been given thought and prayer. Should you receive a "no" answer, don't become discouraged. Take heart that God has in mind the right person and that it will be worth the wait to find someone who can give you a wholehearted "yes."

◆ *Empower others to extend invitations on behalf of the team.* The team leader should not be the only person on the team recruiting new team members. It's in the interest of all the team members to be engaged in this process. Train and release other team members to "go and do likewise."

2. Provide the Tools for Success

Someone has accepted the invitation to join the team and is eager to get started. Think about the last time you started a brand new job. What were some of the steps taken by your manager to help you acclimate to your new place of service and succeed in your new role? Perhaps there was a formal orientation where you were given a tour of the facility and were introduced to your co-workers. Maybe you were asked to take a particular training class or were partnered with someone to show you the ropes. Hopefully, you felt welcomed and supported in your new position. If not, the process of fitting in and contributing was likely a struggle.

People who serve in a volunteer capacity in the church have the same needs you did. They need to feel welcomed and be oriented to the environment in which they will serve. They need to be trained so that they will be competent and confident in their new role. They need to be provided with the resources needed to accomplish the task at hand, whether that resource is space or a budget.

Put yourself in the shoes of your brand new team member and plan to do the following:

◆ *Extend hospitality.* In order to be successful, members of the team need to establish a basis for personal connection. This starts with getting to know one another. Whenever a new person joins an existing team, time must be taken to help them experience being welcomed and to introduce the people already on the team. If you've moved beyond the informal icebreaker questions with the group, you will likely want to go back and revisit these again. You can keep it fresh for all team members by using new questions once you are past the standards of names, church history, and relationships. Take time to revisit your team covenant together as well.

◆ *Provide adequate training.* Ask yourself, what does the new team member need to know in order to accomplish his or her assigned task? Training can be formal or informal. It may be that the team leader needs to spend one-on-one time with the new recruit, working in partnership until responsibilities can be fully transitioned. The leader might also pair the new member with an existing member for a season. In some instances, it might be appropriate to have the new team member read a book or other educational materials relating to the work of the team. In more rare circumstances, team members might be sent to training classes or workshops, especially if specific or technical expertise is needed.

Training has to do with imparting knowledge and skills. Be sure you newest team member has been given enough of both to feel competent for what he or she is being asked to do.

◆ *Supply the necessary resources.* Here you will want to answer the question, "What tools and resources are needed to do the job?" Does fulfilling the responsibilities assigned to the team member require funding? What about facility space? Does the new team member know who to ask to reserve a room at the church or how to get an article in the church bulletin? Does your new team member need access to church office equipment and supplies? The answer can be as simple as knowing where photocopies can be made. There is nothing more frustrating than being clueless about where to go for help. You, or someone on the team, must again try to wear the shoes of the new recruit and walk through the basics of the position.

◆ *Ask for feedback.* You will not know if you have been successful with your hospitality and training efforts unless you ask. Check in with new team members at least once a month and ask how it's going for them. Find out if more help is needed or if serving on this team in their given capacity is proving to be a good fit. If not, you may need to explore together another role on the team or perhaps a different ministry option altogether.

3. Plan for Growth and Renewal

We've already discussed some of the relational implications when team members engage in regular opportunities to learn and grow spiritually together. Serving in the church can be draining, even when we are engaged in Spirit-filled work for which we have a passion. As individuals, we need a plan to recharge our batteries, to experience spiritual growth and renewal in order to avoid burnout. As a leader, you must be proactive in helping others with whom you serve do the same.

This can be tricky. People aren't all wired in the same way, so what refuels me might not refuel my fellow teammate. I might recharge at a large church conference where I can experience high-energy fellowship and a variety of expert speakers. My teammate might find more spiritual vitality in a quiet retreat with the Bible and a good dose of prayer. While there are certain activities the entire team can and should engage in from time-to-time (book studies, regular devotions and prayer, team retreats, training events), you also will need to discern and encourage the best opportunities for growth for your individual team members. There are tangible actions you can take to provide for individual renewal. The following list is not meant to be exhaustive but to seed some ideas. Start with these, and then create your own list:

◆ *Show appreciation.* Being thanked goes a long way toward renewing one's spirits. Send handwritten notes of thanks and encouragement to individual team members. Make these personal and specific to their contributions.

- *Show concern.* If a team member is going through a difficult time, your time and presence can be very meaningful. Visit team members when they are sick, provide them with meals, attend the memorial services of their loved ones, and so forth.
- *Celebrate joys.* It's easy to forget to be there in the good times as well as the bad. Bring a birthday cake to the next team meeting if someone on the team is celebrating a birthday that month. Celebrate a successful accomplishment or the contribution of a team member with an award. You can make up a special certificate and award an inexpensive prize. Get other team members to brainstorm ideas with you.
- *Grant sabbaticals.* There are seasons in life and in ministry. We need to be willing to allow someone with challenging life circumstances to step away for a season without inducing feelings of guilt. When able, this individual will rejoin the team with more enthusiasm and commitment for the work of the ministry.
- *Share books.* Are you aware of an area of development one of your team members has targeted for personal growth? This could relate to a spiritual discipline such as prayer or to a skill such as personal communication. Is there a book on this topic on your bookshelf collecting dust? Why not dust it off and let the team member benefit from its contents? If the budget allows, purchase a new book.
- *Send your people to a training event.* Not all events are cost prohibitive. Recognize the payoff for these types of investments. Churches benefit from the new ideas and skills that come from revitalized members attending such events. Find a balance between good stewardship of church resources and investing in people and the future of the church.
- *Provide a place for a spiritual retreat.* Does your church conference own a retreat property? Perhaps there are such facilities affiliated with other churches in your immediate area. If so, consider giving the gift of a night or two away at a retreat center for your team members, individually or collectively.

Again, this list is certainly not exhaustive. It is meant to fuel your own thoughts and ideas about ways in which you, as a leader, can be intentional about encouraging the personal growth and renewal of the people who serve with you in ministry. The impact of such an investment on the individual, the team, and the work you are about can be substantial. Be sure you also model renewal and growth in your own life. It will be hard for others to accept their limitations (and thus the need for renewal and growth) if their leader does not appear to have any limitations of his or her own.

Seeking a Mentor

Consider developing a relationship with a mentor, someone who is further down the path than you in the area of team-building who will help you take your learning to the next level. You will ultimately need to live into the concepts in this book on your own, but you can gain a greater depth of understanding on a practical level by learning from the experience of someone who is already successful at what you are attempting to do.

Identify someone in your church who is already a great team leader. (If you cannot think of someone inside the church, look outside—perhaps a someone who is a successful business, community, or civic leader.) Contact this individual and share with him or her the desire you have to become an effective team leader. Set up a time to meet, perhaps over coffee or lunch. Taking into account what you have read in this chapter, write down some questions to find out the person's perspective on what makes him or her successful at leading a team. Bring your list of questions to your meeting, but be sure to allow ample time for listening to the person's thoughts and ideas. Ask if he or she is open to having future discussions. After the meeting, be sure to send the individual a handwritten thank you note.

It's Worth the Effort

We began this chapter stating the importance to leaders of developing team-building skills. Why? Effective leaders recognize they were not meant to be the doers of all ministry; they know they have a crucial role in inviting, equipping, and releasing others to contribute meaningful service as well. Kingdom impact is multiplied exponentially through leaders who are successful team builders. Team ministry is an expression of the body of Christ in action—people with diverse gifts unified around a common purpose, with each part contributing to the whole.

Developing and then practicing these skills takes time, intentional effort, and patience. So often it seems easier to just do what needs to be done ourselves. We like having control over the outcome. Those of us who operate in a team environment on a regular basis recognize the challenges. We lose team members and have to start the process of inviting all over again. Getting a group of people to bond and then work together harmoniously often slows down work on a project, at least initially. Perhaps you are able to conjure up your own arguments against teams.

> # Developing and then practicing these skills takes time, intentional effort, and patience.

If you have ever experienced serving on a healthy and productive team, you won't need to be convinced. Your motivation to develop team-building skills will come from a deep desire to maximize your impact to serve Christ and others, because you will know beyond a shadow of a doubt that whatever you can accomplish alone will pale in comparison to the impact a team of committed servants can have. Plus, investing yourself in the development of others is a rewarding experience, one that will bring you great joy. Now, all that's left for you to do is to roll up your sleeves and get started!

Questions for Reflection or Discussion

1. Identify a team-building skill you are already proficient in using. What makes this the case? What is something simple you can do to further use this skill in your leadership?

2. What is the greatest obstacle you face in becoming an effective team builder? How will you overcome this obstacle?

3. If you were to pick just one team-building skill to begin developing, what would it be? Write it down, along with at least three action steps for practicing this skill.

CHAPTER 4

Meetings That Work

Let us consider how to provoke one another to love and good deeds, not neglecting to meet together. (Hebrews 10:24-25a)

I (Yvonne) attend a lot of meetings—meetings at work, meetings at church, even meetings to talk about meetings! Some of them are productive and exciting, but too many of them seem like a complete waste of time. You've probably experienced the same frustration occasionally.

One of the primary responsibilities of a leader is facilitation—whether facilitating meetings or Bible studies or some other kind of gathering of people. For a few leaders, this comes naturally. For others of us, though, it can be a daunting task. Where do you begin? How do you prepare? What if things don't go the way you planned? (By the way, you can count on this happening!)

Facilitation doesn't have to be overwhelming, and every meeting has the potential to be a satisfying and worthwhile use of time. In this chapter we provide you with some tips and tools to make the process more manageable and the experience more enjoyable for everyone involved.

What Makes a Meeting Good or Bad?

You probably don't have a list you can recite off the top of your head, but my guess is that if you spend a few minutes thinking about some of the good and some of the bad meetings you've participated in, you can identify a few characteristics that contributed positively or negatively to the experience. For instance, in a good meeting, typically many or all people present actively participate. On the other hand, if one person does all the talking in the meeting (even the leader), it's usually a less positive experience for the rest of the group.

Ponder for a moment the "bad" meetings you've attended. What happened? Why were the experiences frustrating or unpleasant?

Now think about some of the "good" meetings. What made the experiences good?

It's helpful to spend time considering this, because a pattern does start to emerge. Did you notice that you ended up with opposites in your lists of characteristics? This pattern gives you great insight regarding how to make your meetings better, because it helps you understand what you should be sure to include and what you should try to avoid at all costs. In fact, with a little planning and preparation, you can make every meeting more productive and enjoyable.

Let's look at some of the most commonly mentioned characteristics of good and bad meetings:

GOOD	*BAD*
Has a clearly defined purpose	Seems to be pointless
People connect with one another	Leaves no time for personal interaction
Everyone participates	One person (or a few people) dominates
Uses effective time management	Gets off track or just seems to last forever!
Uses an agenda as a guideline	Has no agenda or agenda over rides people's needs
Has clearly stated action plans for after the meeting	No action plan or "take away"
Encourages and cares for attendees	Attendees are "means to an end" – worker bees

Using the tools and tips that follow in the rest of this chapter, you will be able to avoid some of the pitfalls that lead to dissatisfying meetings, and to ensure that you include the facets that lead to successful meetings.

Planning a Productive Meeting

Every successful meeting starts with a plan. For simplicity's sake, we're going to refer to this as the "agenda." If you're leading a Bible study, this actually will be a "lesson plan," but the same concepts apply to developing a lesson plan as to developing a plan for leading a business meeting.

An agenda serves as an outline for the meeting, but in reality it is much more. A properly constructed agenda should contain the following elements:

◆ clearly defined purpose for the meeting
◆ opening
◆ connection activity—designed to engage and connect the participants
◆ prayer
◆ review of the last meeting (if needed)/meeting purpose and end time
◆ content—the agenda items or discussion outline, if leading a Bible study
◆ closing

◆ summary
◆ review of action items
◆ next meeting date/time
◆ recognition
◆ joys and concerns/closing prayer
◆ time-markers and speaker assignments for each section

Let's discuss each of these points in more detail. An outline for you to use in developing your agenda each time you plan a meeting is provided in the Appendix (p. 118).

Clearly Defined Purpose for the Meeting

With this in mind, we constantly pray for you, that our God may count you worthy of his calling, and that by his power he may fulfill every good purpose of yours and every act prompted by your faith. (2 Thessalonians 1:11, NIV)

This is a critical step. You need a clearly defined and easily communicated vision of the desired outcome of the meeting. If you can't clearly define the purpose of the meeting (What do I hope to accomplish, or what is the key learning?), don't have a meeting. Let me state that again: If you can't clearly define the purpose of the meeting, don't have one! The purpose of the meeting can be complex, or quite simple. Perhaps your purpose is to develop a strategic plan for your ministry area. It might be to plan an upcoming social event. If you're leading a Bible study, your purpose will be related to the key learning points you want participants to take away from the lesson. Whatever it is, if you're going to have a meeting, you need to define it, because the rest of your plan for the meeting will flow from this purpose.

Opening

Day by day, as they spent much time together in the temple, they broke bread at home and ate their food with glad and generous hearts, praising God and having the goodwill of all the people. (Acts 2:46-47)

Connection Activity

One of the hallmarks of a successful meeting is active participation by all of the people present. An effective method of kick-starting participation is to get people talking to one another early in the meeting. The longer someone is in a meeting without speaking, the more likely he or she is to leave the meeting without ever speaking. You want to get everyone engaged and feeling included from the very beginning. Ice-breakers are a quick and effective tool for accomplishing this goal.

Now, before you start rolling your eyes at the thought of doing ice-breakers, keep in mind that everyone rolls their eyes when you announce that you're going to do an ice-breaker. Therefore, you never want to announce it—just do it! On the agenda, you might simply list it as "Connect." Either plan a short activity, or have a couple of simple questions prepared for people to consider and respond to within the group.

Three years ago, Carol and I started a new small group. The purpose of this small group was spiritual growth in the context of authentic Christian community. It was a mixed group—all ages, mixed backgrounds, varying levels of spiritual maturity. Some of us knew one another, but most did not. We planned structured ice-breakers every week for the first six weeks. The first ones we did were very non-threatening activities designed to help us learn more about one another and laugh at the same time. After the six weeks, we still had (and still have) an informal "connection" time when we share what's happening in our weeks and just catch up. I'm convinced these kinds of activities set the stage for a dynamic, relational group.

There are a number of great resources for ice-breakers available, including several websites specifically related to ice-breaker activities. One of my favorite resources is a book called *Ice-Breakers and Heart-Warmers* by Steve Sheely (Serendipity House, 1996). See the Appendix (p. 119) for a few ice-breakers you can use.

Prayer

An opening prayer serves as a transition to the "meat" of the meeting. It doesn't have to be long or even eloquent, but it *is necessary*. No gathering of believers for official ministry purposes or social events should begin without inviting God's presence and giving thanks for the work God has done through and among the group. If you're not comfortable praying extemporaneously, you can read a prayer you wrote earlier or a prayer from a book of prayers or the Bible.

Review of the Last Meeting/Meeting Purpose and End Time

Reviewing the last meeting and reading aloud the purpose of this meeting and the time allotted for it serves two purposes: it keeps participants focused on the topic at hand, and it lets them know there will eventually be an end to the meeting. (Okay, we are just kidding.) Seriously, letting people know you want to honor their time and will let them go at the stated end time helps them engage in the meeting. If you have a habit of keeping your meetings on schedule, people will be more willing to attend them.

Content

Now to him who by the power at work within us is able to accomplish abundantly far more than all we can ask or imagine, to him be glory in the church and in Christ Jesus to all generations, forever and ever. Amen. (Ephesians 3:20-21)

This section of the meeting is the primary point of the gathering, whether it is the Bible study and discussion or the topics for discussion. Keep it simple. If there are too many topics for discussion, you are better off breaking them into multiple meetings. For every agenda item, you need to consider four things ahead of time: the desired outcome, how you will achieve that outcome, the time needed for discussion, and the person who will introduce the topic.

Let's use an initial meeting to plan an upcoming pool party as an example. My agenda items might include date/time, location, food, and entertainment, among others. The desired outcome answers the question, "What do I need to accomplish by discussing this topic?" So, in our pool party example, our desired outcome for discussing the date/time of the party is simply to pick a date and time. I, as the leader of the meeting, will initiate the discussion by suggesting a couple of dates and times. Then the group can reach consensus on one that works for all or most people present. The decision can be reached in just a couple of minutes.

> **If you have a habit of keeping your meetings on schedule, people will be more willing to attend them.**

As you consider each agenda item, decide how to best reach your desired outcome. Some items may be reports requiring little or no discussion; some topics may require the generating of ideas, which may come best through brainstorming; and some decisions may need to be reached by a vote. The key is to decide this ahead of time. It is also critical to decide (through volunteers or assignments) who will assume responsibility for any actions that need to be taken on each item, as well as the time frame for accomplishing the actions. Otherwise you may end up discussing all the topics but reaching conclusions about nothing.

For a Bible study, you should consider what questions to ask in order to cover your desired learning points, and then decide whether you want to discuss each topic, as a full group, to break up into smaller groups for some parts of the discussion, or even to pair up with discussion partners for some topics for a change of pace. Make sure the questions are open-ended—not answerable with a "yes" or "no" response.

Closing

Let love be genuine…love one another with mutual affection; outdo one another in showing honor. Do not lag in zeal, be ardent in spirit, serve the Lord. Rejoice in hope, be patient in suffering, persevere in prayer. ...Rejoice with those who rejoice, weep with those who weep. (Romans 12:9a, 10-12,15)

As your meeting draws to a close, provide a summary of the decisions made, what action is to be taken, who is responsible for that action, and the time frame or deadline for the action to be completed. Decide when and where your next meeting will be held, and review the items that will be included on the agenda—or, if you are leading a Bible study, the topic you'll be studying and discussing in the next session. This is also an ideal time for thanking the group for work they have done, celebrating any accomplishments or milestones reached by the group, and recognizing individuals for a job well done or special events in their lives. Finally, end by asking for joys and concerns from the attendees and then saying a closing prayer.

Time Limits and Speaker Assignments

Setting a general time limit for each agenda item will help determine whether you can accomplish your goals within this meeting time or whether you need to hold multiple meetings. This is especially important when you are trying to decide what to include and not include in a Bible study discussion. If you aren't certain about the timing, you might want to mark those questions in your lesson plan that are most important to discuss and then get to the others as time allows. A time limit also will help you keep the meeting on track so you can finish within the time allotted.

As we mentioned earlier, good meetings typically elicit the participation of everyone in attendance. It is beneficial, therefore, if others initiate and participate in the discussion of some of the agenda items. If you're the only one talking, you should have just sent an e-mail and saved everyone the time and trouble of a meeting. Before the meeting date, ask others who will be attending to start the discussion for specific agenda items.

Facilitating the Meeting

The act of facilitating is defined as "to make easy" or "to bring about." Facilitating a meeting or a Bible study is about making a discussion flow more smoothly. Sometimes we confuse facilitating with teaching. Teaching, however, is imparting knowledge. In facilitation, you don't need to have the answers—you're supposed to have the questions! A facilitator functions somewhat like a traffic cop—asking questions to get the conversation moving, and redirecting or stopping the flow of traffic to avoid a roadblock or traffic jam. In this section we provide some tips and tools to do just that; but first, let's talk about something that always overrides your planned agenda: an individual's urgent need.

Although a facilitator is supposed to keep things moving and on schedule, as leaders we must always make people our primary focus. If someone comes to your gathering with an urgent need, you need to be prepared to shift focus immediately and either provide help or identify the care that is needed. You might ask the group to pray for the individual and then ask someone to take over the meeting while you step outside the meeting room to assist the person requiring care. As a leader, you need to carry with you the contact information for the pastors or other caregivers at your church—specifically for instances like this. If you don't feel competent to care for the person, call someone who is. Whatever you do, don't ignore the person's need, and don't downplay it, sending him or her home without making sure that the crisis has passed and that someone will follow up.

Whether you are facilitating a Bible study or team meeting, once the discussion begins, try following the ACTS model of facilitation to keep things going:

A cknowledge every person who speaks during a discussion.
C larify what is being expressed, or ask for clarification if needed.
T ake the comments to the group as a means of generating discussion.
S ummarize what has been said.

(*Leading Life-Changing Small Groups*, Bill Donahue, Zondervan Publishing, 1996, p. 112)

Sometimes, though, the discussion just doesn't seem to flow smoothly. Let's look at a few challenges commonly faced by facilitators.

What If Nobody Speaks Up?

Be prepared for silence when you ask the first question. People are sometimes intimidated about speaking up first. Sometimes they're afraid they'll embarrass themselves with a "wrong answer." You can avoid this issue by asking for opinions, thoughts, or feelings on a topic as opposed to an outright answer. Even if an ice-breaker helped to warm up the group, sometimes the first question is still met with silence. Wait for a while. Eventually, someone will be unable to bear the silence any longer and will speak up. If not, try rephrasing the question or asking one member of the group to share his or her views.

What If One Member in Particular Is Quiet?

Most groups have one or two members who are more reserved than others. They may be shy, bored, tired, or disengaged. If you're leading a Bible study, try asking them to read a passage of Scripture aloud. If you're in a business meeting, you might considering asking (prior to the meeting) a more reserved person to be the note taker or fill some other role to keep him or her engaged. After others in the group have offered their perspectives, ask quiet members if they have an opinion to share or anything to add. Often quiet members will share if they can do it in smaller groups, so you might try pairing people up to discuss something and then report back to the group.

What If One Member Tries to Dominate the Discussion?

Sometimes the person dominating the conversation thinks he or she is being helpful by filling the silence, and typically the person isn't even aware how much he or she is monopolizing the floor. Acknowledge the person's contribution and then redirect the conversation ("Thanks, Debi. Does someone else have something to add?"). You can summarize what the person has said and then change topics. Attempt indirectly to shift the focus away from the dominator, if possible, but be direct if you have difficulty getting your point across ("Thanks for sharing, Tina. Let's give someone else a chance to contribute. Marianne, what are your thoughts on this subject?").

How Do I Get the Group Back on Topic?

Great discussions often lead us slightly (or completely) off the original topic. Sometimes this is fine, but at other times it's important to bring the focus back to the original topic. Redirect the group by acknowledging that the discussion has strayed, restating the original topic, and asking a question. If appropriate and time allows, take a quick break and refocus the conversation as you regroup. If the new discussion direction is important but time won't allow you to continue to explore it, "park it." Tell the group it's important but you'll have to discuss it at your next meeting.

How Do I Handle a Know-it-all?

Occasionally you'll experience a group member who thinks he or she has it all figured out. This person is eager to share what he or she knows as if it's gospel truth, even in the face of dissenting opinions. Keep in mind that it's important to honor the individual's feelings as you redirect the discussion. If appropriate, lovingly defend your ground, presenting support for your position. Encourage the group to recognize that experience informs interpretation, and that people will have different perspectives based on their experiences. You can frequently avoid an argument simply by acknowledging the person's perspective and agreeing to disagree.

Using an Agenda Template

Let's practice preparing for a meeting. For the sake of this exercise, we'll use the purpose of planning an upcoming pool party for our ministry team or small group. Using the agenda template in the Appendix (p. 118), complete an agenda as if you were leading the meeting.

What ice-breaker will you use? What are the agenda items in your content section? Which ones can you reach a decision on at this meeting, and how will you do so? What will you do with the others? (Perhaps you'll need to ask for volunteers to serve on a sub-committee to do research and report back to the group.)

What are the action steps? Based on the date of the pool party, what are the deadlines for completion of these action steps?

Preparing for your meeting in advance will do a lot to help you facilitate the discussion. Some leaders prepare the agenda by simply putting the topics to be discussed on a piece of paper, giving little thought to timing, methods of decision-making, or involving others. Using an agenda template and the facilitation tips in this chapter will make your meetings more productive and enjoyable for everyone in attendance—including you! The upfront work will ease your tension and help you feel equipped for leading the discussion.

Questions for Reflection or Discussion

1. Discuss the characteristics of the best and worst meetings you've attended. No names, please! What will you do as you lead your next meeting to model the best meeting and avoid the problems you experienced in the worst meeting?

2. What aspect of facilitation do you struggle with the most? What resources or tools can you use to compensate for that?

3. Reflect on the last meeting you led. What things would you repeat and what would you change to make it better next time?

Developing Vision, Mission, and Values Statements

Where there is no vision, the people perish. (Proverbs 29:18a KJV)

What difference does it make to know where you are going, what you are going to do, and who you want to be in your life? I (Carol) have one daughter already in college and another in decision mode, getting ready to choose the schools with which she will begin the application process. In the case of Lauren, who is already attending college, the year leading up to making her decision was filled with anxiety, frustration, and a few tears. At the outset, Lauren wasn't sure what she wanted to do with the rest of her life, and until that became clear, it was difficult to make choices about where to go and what to do once she was there.

Figuring out the answers to those questions involved reflection and research. The process included giving thought to how God designed her and what God's will for her life might be. Once she discovered this, taking action toward her life goals not only became easier but also made decisions exciting and joyful. Lauren determined she was gifted at science and learning foreign languages, and she made the decision to major in both chemistry and Spanish. She then researched and applied to schools known for having good programs in her chosen fields of study. One year later, she is well on her way to realizing her dreams for her life.

Lauren's having a sense of direction was almost as important to her father and me as it was to her, for it potentially meant the difference between graduating in four years versus six. Yes, we're talking resource implications here! It is also much easier for us to encourage and support her when we have clarity about the goals she has for her future. This clarity serves to motivate Lauren to keep moving forward when she experiences challenges or the reality of the hard work it takes to accomplish her goals.

Perhaps the memories of your college days are still fresh in your mind. You either entered school with absolute certainty about what you hoped to achieve or you floundered for a while until you found your way. College students will often change majors at some point, but having that initial direction keeps them from floundering indefinitely. The same is true for us. There are times we step out in faith in a direction we feel God is leading us, giving ourselves permission for a change later should God redirect our path.

Just as it is important for us as individuals to have a clear sense of direction, purpose, and behavior, so also it is important for the churches we serve and the specific ministries we represent. This involves defining—for others and for ourselves—our vision, mission, and values.

The purpose of this chapter is to provide you with the tools you need to create a vision statement, a mission statement, and a values statement for a ministry or team. Simply put, a vision statement captures in writing a picture of the preferable future and gives the organization or individual direction. A mission statement, also sometimes called a purpose statement, defines why you exist and what you do. Values speak to character and define who we are and how we behave when we are at our very best. Together, vision, mission, and values create a framework within which we can operate, provide inspiration and motivation to work together toward the realization of our goals, and set a standard from which we can measure our effectiveness. They must align with God's vision, be grounded in the Scriptures, and communicated with clarity and regularity.

Learning From Past Experience

Before we move into the steps of creating vision, mission, and values statements, it might be helpful to engage in reflection on your personal experiences involving these. Think back to a time when you were involved with a specific project that meets the following criteria: it progressed successfully, provided you with ongoing enthusiasm and motivation, and generally achieved the desired results. Once you have the project in mind, answer the following questions:

◆ What was the project, and what motivated you to join the effort toward completing it?

◆ What specifically was communicated to you about the nature and work of the project, and how?

◆ What specific role did you play in contributing to the project? While working on the project, what brought you the greatest joy? What frustrated you?

◆ How did you measure success? How did you know you had accomplished what you set out to do?

If answering the above questions was easy for you, chances are that the project, and your role in supporting it, had a clear focus. If you found this to be a challenging exercise, it may be because you lacked clarity. Either way, we hope that you are motivated to learn all you can to provide absolute direction and purpose to those you lead.

Vision Statement—An Inspirational Painting of the Future

A vision statement captures in words a picture depicting the future. It also conveys a present reality as it is being lived into. A vision statement describes a positive, hopeful state of being. It provides direction and describes where we are heading.

Perhaps one of the most famous examples of a preferred future vision can be found in Dr. Martin Luther King, Jr.'s "I Have a Dream" speech. His speech was forceful, filled with passion and emotion. It stirred something in the soul of every listener who shared King's desire that his children would "one day live in a nation where they will not be judged by the color of their skin but by the content of their character." Worthy visions do that—they move and engage us. They inspire us to action.

As a leader, you need to be aware of three levels of vision. First, you should be operating in harmony with the vision of your organization, or the church. If you are the most senior leader of your church, you are responsible for helping the entire church body live into the vision as well. Second, you need either to craft or uphold the vision for the particular ministry area you represent. This vision should be in alignment with the overall vision of the church and provide greater specificity to the ministry team. Finally, you should have a personal vision statement—one that aligns with your individual gifts and passion. This third vision statement helps you to hold true to the personal calling you have received from God. It serves as a decision-making tool you can use when faced with a myriad of choices, bringing focus to your work.

For the purpose of this chapter, we will focus our attention on the crafting of a team or ministry vision statement. If your church has a vision statement, your role as a ministry team leader will be one of communication and alignment. The ministry you represent, and the people who serve on your team, will need to operate in harmony with the church vision. If your church does not have a vision statement, you might start by asking questions. Does your church have a vision that is not explicit, yet everyone knows the direction the church is heading? If this is the case, visit with your senior leadership about capturing the vision in writing. This is the statement you will want to begin with as you develop the vision for your ministry.

Write the vision statement of your church here:

If possible, try to learn the history behind your church's vision—the when, who, where, and why behind its creation. A vision statement for the church, a ministry area of the church, or even an individual leader in the church should align with the Scriptures. In the space that follows, write the ways in which the vision of your church does so:

Now it is time to thoughtfully and prayerfully try your hand at crafting a vision statement for your particular ministry. You may be wondering if you should undertake this assignment on your own, especially since you know that you need the buy-in of everyone who contributes to the ministry in order for the ministry to be successful. The answer is both yes and no.

Yes, because you need to practice so that you can begin to hone your skill at developing a vision statement. Yes, because rarely are such statements created in groups. A vision statement is generally the work of the most senior leader of the ministry, although it can be assigned to another leader who is heavily involved.

No, because there will be ways to involve others who are stakeholders in the ministry, such as the members of your team or committee, in the process. For example, you might ask each person on the team to write three sentences he or she would use to describe the ministry five years from now. Ask them to describe what will be different in the life of the church or community, or in individuals' lives, as a result of the work of the team.

Pray privately over the lists created by your team members, and then write a draft of a vision statement. Once your draft statement is ready, bring it back to the team for their prayers, final input, wordsmithing, and approval.

Use the "Vision Statement Writing Tool" in the Appendix (p. 124) to practice writing a ministry vision statement.

Once you have your draft completed, you will want to evaluate what you have written by asking the following questions:

◆ Does it adequately paint a picture of what is hoped for the future? *(Consider the apostle John and the revelation given to him of a new heaven and a new earth. See Revelation 21.)*

◆ Is the direction the picture provides clear to all who read it? *(Consider Nehemiah and the rebuilding of the walls of Jerusalem. See Nehemiah 2:1–3:32.)*

◆ Will it inspire anyone to take steps toward making the vision a reality? *(Consider Moses inspiring the people to leave Egypt and venture across a vast desert toward a promised land flowing with milk and honey. See Exodus 12:33-50.)*

◆ Is it challenging enough to require dependence on God? *(Consider Esther going before the king in an attempt to save her people from certain destruction. See Esther 4.)*

◆ Does it align with what we know of God's will and with Scripture? *(Consider Jesus and his absolute resolve to do the will of his Father. See John 14:1-14.)*

◆ Will it outlive us? *(Consider Abraham and the vision that his descendants would be as numerous as the stars. See Genesis 15:1-6.)*

If you cannot answer "yes" to each of these questions, go back to the drawing board. An effective vision statement will unite hearts, minds, and muscle. People will invest heavily with their resources and time once they are on board with the vision. This means the vision must be compelling. Visions also should exist for the common good — for the benefit of others, not for the benefit of the leader or the ministry itself.

Once you have a written vision statement, it will be your responsibility to communicate it to others. Use it in your written communications and post it on your website. Keep it visible for all you hope to involve in the ministry. After a season, you should be able to share stories of tangible ways in which the vision is being lived and realized.

Vision statements rarely, if ever, change. This is due largely to the nature of what they are — a prayerful, thoughtful, God-inspired picture of the future. What may change are the strategies and tactics for achieving your vision and mission. We'll move now to developing a mission statement and take a look at strategic planning in chapter 6.

Mission Statement — The Purpose for Our Existence

In broad terms, a mission statement captures the "big picture" purpose for our existence. It includes elements that convey who we are, what we do, and why we do it. Like vision statements, mission statements should be prayerfully and thoughtfully crafted in alignment with the Scriptures. A simple way to view the topic is to think of a mission statement as our "marching orders." The vision points us to a destination; the mission tells us how to get there. As was the case with vision, leaders should consider the mission of the church, the mission of each particular ministry, and their own personal mission.

In chapter 3 we referred to the benefits of a well-crafted mission statement in relationship to team-building, but it is worthwhile to review the benefits here as well. In a nutshell, a mission statement should help your church, your ministry team, and you to

◆ understand what the team is supposed to do and why — and what it should *not* do

◆ appreciate the importance of the team's role within the community or church

◆ evaluate challenges and celebrate successes

◆ communicate the work of the team to others outside the team

◆ focus its creativity, efforts, energy, and thinking

The mission statement of a ministry or team must align with the mission statement (sometimes referred to as purpose statement) of the church. The mission of the ministry in which a leader chooses to invest his or her heart, mind, and strength also should be harmonious with that leader's personal mission statement. As with the vision statement, if your church does not have a written mission statement, work with your senior leadership to create one. (If you do not have a personal mission statement, use the tools and format presented on page 125 in the Appendix to write one. A personal mission statement should take into account your gifts and passions and answer the question "What purpose does God have for my life?")

An effective mission statement for a church or team will create unity of purpose, clarity of tasks, and a sense of community among those working to accomplish it. Unlike the vision statement, which is primarily crafted by one or a few leaders, the entire ministry team will be involved in both crafting its mission statement and revisiting it annually—as well as each time someone new joins the team.

If after reading chapter 3 you did not draft a mission statement for a ministry in which you are involved, use the worksheet in the Appendix (p. 120) to do so now. Write your final mission statement in the space that follows:

Write the mission or purpose statement of your church here:

Evaluate the ministry mission statement against the mission statement of the church. Are the two in alignment? If not, what might you change about your ministry mission statement so that it supports the mission of the church?

Values Statement—A Reflection of Character and Behavior

In chapter 1, we considered personal values as integral to the way we live our lives and set an example for others. Our values define our character and our behavior. The same is true of organizational values. When a church defines her values, she is making a statement about who she is and how she behaves when at her very best. When we capture values on paper, on behalf of our church or our ministries, we are communicating those characteristics and behaviors we consider to be non-negotiable. We should strive to live into our values consistently—not just when the urge strikes us.

Creating a values statement for a church or particular ministry should be a team effort. Writing a church values statement should involve the senior pastor, the church's governing council, and perhaps other key staff or lay leaders. Creating a values statement for a ministry area should involve key leaders of the ministry. Lists of values can become exhaustive. I (Carol) have been in brainstorming sessions where a group of people generated a list of over thirty ministry values. It is a good idea to narrow the list to ten or fewer, because any more than that will be difficult to communicate and manage. Values statements are tools for designing, implementing, and evaluating ministry. If the list is too long, it becomes cumbersome and overwhelming.

One method for narrowing the list is to give each participant in the brainstorming meeting three to five votes, instructing them to place a checkmark next to their top choices for inclusion on the final list. Once the votes are tallied, add the top choices to the draft statement. At that point, the group should reach final consensus with regard to the number of values to list.

It is very likely that every value you and your church will want to consider may be found in the Bible. For some great inspiration, take time to read Matthew 5-7; Galatians 5:22-23; Romans 12:1; Corinthians 13; Ephesians 4; Philippians 4:8; and 1 Timothy 3-4. Other sources for determining values might include church history and tradition, a trusted authority figure such as a pastor, and past experiences. The values these sources suggest should also be consistent with Scripture. Remember, the core values of your church and your ministries are central to their identity. It is important that they are a true reflection of who you are—both now and in the future.

In the Appendix (p. 127) you will find a sample values statement given by one church as an example to their small groups. Groups are provided this list but are instructed to discuss and create a list of values with the input of all the members of the group. For the small groups, their values are a key component of their group covenant. The list should reflect the character and behavioral expectations of the group members individually and collectively. In the case of the small group, members are inviting one another to hold them accountable. All group decisions are to be made in light of the group's values.

Try your hand at creating a ministry values statement using the worksheet in the Appendix (p. 128). Be sure to consider the character and behavior attributes that will give the ministry its identity.

Reality Check—Making Vision, Mission, and Values Count

The exercise of creating vision, mission, and values statements is time-consuming and often challenging work. Your effort will have been for naught unless you use these tools to inspire people to action and hold yourself and your ministry accountable for results. Failing to do what we say we are going to do also results in loss of credibility.

How do we avoid this? Quite simply, by conducting periodic assessments. If you wish to determine the clarity of your vision and mission, ask your key leaders or team members. Take time during a regularly scheduled meeting and ask everyone to write the vision, mission, or values of the ministry on a slip of paper. If this proves to be too difficult, you need to step up your efforts to communicate and reinforce these statements.

Another way to assess effectiveness is to evaluate the use of budget and people resources. Are ministry resources actually being allocated toward work that fulfills the mission of the ministry? Is the ministry team actually doing the work that is described in the mission statement? Is the ministry achieving tangible results with regard to its vision? What examples can you list of team members exemplifying the character or behavior captured in the values statement? If you do not get affirming responses to these questions, you need to change either your work or your vision, mission, and values.

> **Worthwhile visions always drive us to our knees. There is an element to them that overwhelms.**

A Shared Destiny

Michelangelo said, "Lord, grant that I may always desire more than I can accomplish." There is something to be said for having a vision larger than what can be realized by mere mortals. Worthwhile visions always drive us to our knees. There is an element to them that overwhelms. Such visions frequently require change, which often leads to a measure of discomfort.

A captivating mission motivates us to action. If we know with certainty that the work we do, with God's help, makes a difference in the world, we are more willing to give ourselves away in order to see it through to completion. Hard work does not deter us.

Serving God with Christ-like character—acting as salt and light in the world—draws people to our churches and ministries and, ultimately, to God. Using the Bible as our guidebook for accomplishing the work of ministry gives us a framework within which to operate. As we strive to live into biblical values, we grow in our understanding of what it means to be true disciples of Christ.

The goal is to enroll others in the work of the church and then to operate in harmony with God's plans and in unity with one another. Leaders help others develop a shared sense of destiny as they articulate the vision, mission, and values of the church and its ministries. Once clearly mapped, these must be communicated with passion and frequency—not only by the leader but also by others who are committed to the ministry. Is it not amazing and humbling to know that God entrusts God's work to our human hands? If that is the case, then is this work not worth our very best efforts to enlist others to see the vision, live the mission, and model the values?

Questions for Reflection or Discussion

1. Think of a visionary leader you were inspired to follow. What made his or her vision worthy of following?

2. Read or listen to an inspirational speech, such as one given by Dr. King or another visionary leader, by searching online or visiting a local library. What about the speech works to ignite passion or inspire action?

3. Think back to a time when you were influenced by a television or print advertisement to make a significant purchase. Describe in detail what about the ad inspired you to action. How might you apply those same principles to creating and communicating an influential mission statement?

4. Search online or check out library resources for effective and memorable mission statements. For example, the mission statement for Walt Disney was simply "to make people happy." Make a list of others you find, and then describe what makes them work or not work.

5. Do the values that businesses represent have any influence on whether or not you become a customer? Why or why not? How might the values upheld by a ministry affect a person's decision to make a commitment to serve or participate in the ministry?

6. Make a list of a few businesses that you frequent on a regular basis. Try to list each company's values based upon your experiences. Next time you visit, ask an employee if the business has written values, and if so, if you may have a copy. Compare their list to your personal list, along with the lists your team members created.

CHAPTER 6

Strategic Planning

"All this, in writing at the LORD's direction, he made clear to me — the plan of all the works." (1 Chronicles 28:19)

My husband and I (Carol) have a few dreams for our future. Some of our goals are quite specific in nature, such as contributing toward our daughters' college educations, preparing for retirement, purchasing a modest home in the country with a fishing pond, and giving money to charitable causes near and dear to our hearts.

While realizing any of our dreams and visions for the future will take intentional actions on our part, there are some life goals that require a formal strategic planning process that includes time-specific and measurable strategies and action steps. We have recognized, for instance, that we must set aside a certain percentage (measurable) of our yearly (time specific) income in preparation for the days we will retire from our current positions in the workforce. An alternative approach to retirement planning might be to hope that between Social Security and our daughters, our financial needs will be met. That scenario does not inspire a great deal of confidence! We do want to realize our dreams.

Strategic planning also has its place in the church. Just as our retirement plans flow from the vision we have for the future, so also a church's strategic plans will flow from the vision it has for the future. The work you have just completed in chapter 5 on vision, mission, and values statements will serve as a foundation for what you are about to undertake.

Lest you think strategic planning is not a spiritual endeavor, and is perhaps too "corporate" for the church, you might want to turn to the Bible and read the Old Testament Book of Nehemiah. It is a good study in the art of prayerful preparation, planning, execution, and the completion of a specific project — the reconstruction of the walls surrounding Jerusalem. Like any worthwhile vision, Nehemiah's plan went beyond the restoration of brick and mortar — it was about the restoration of God's people.

We have a big-picture, master-planner God, but also a detail-oriented God. Consider the specificity of the plans God gave to Noah for the construction of the ark in Genesis 6. Think about the level of detail of God's instructions for the tabernacle beginning in Exodus 25. Reflect on Solomon's plans for God's temple in Jerusalem, which we read beginning in 1 Kings 5.

Strategic planning, done right, is a God-honoring endeavor. We give thought and priority to the visions God has for our churches. We use the tools we have been given to keep our ministries moving toward the specific goal

God has in mind. This chapter will guide you through a proven process that, once mastered, will make your work more effective.

We'll start the process with learning about setting objectives, which are the overarching statements of what we hope to accomplish. Then we'll move into strategies, which help us define our approach to reaching our goals. Finally, we'll break the strategies into manageable-sized chunks, called action steps. We will also discuss strategic planning sessions—what they look like, who you invite, and what you do in the pre-planning, planning, and post-planning stages. Let's get started.

Setting the Objectives

You have a God-given vision, a picture of the future, for your ministry. How will you begin to realize this vision? There is a saying, "A failure to plan is a plan to fail." A good plan starts with a well-stated objective. A simple definition of an objective is "the ends we wish to accomplish in a specified time frame." A properly stated objective will

- ◆ clearly state the desired result
- ◆ be measurable and time specific
- ◆ paint a picture of a point in the future
- ◆ be critical to the success of your ministry
- ◆ move you beyond the normal day-to-day operations of the church

For example, perhaps a church or ministry has a vision for reaching the people in your community who do not have a church home. This church might set an objective as follows: *By January 1, 2008 (time specific), of the people from our community who were previously without a church home (critical to success), 100 will have become members of our church family (measurable).* An example of an objective that does not meet the above criteria might be: *People without a church home will join our church.*

How many objectives should a church or ministry set? Keep it manageable. Too many objectives will overwhelm the people and resources of the church. Strategic objectives also involve ministry that is above and beyond the day-to-day operational requirements of the church or ministry. If you are working toward creating worship that is more visitor-friendly, you do not stop doing the work of planning your weekly worship services.

Most churches will limit the number of church-wide objectives to five or less. Individual ministry areas will often set only one or two. That it is why it is so important to give careful thought to these objectives. You will also need the buy-in of key leaders. The governing body of the church should set church-wide objectives. The staff and/or key leaders of a particular ministry should set that ministry area's objectives. The circles of people involved will widen as the process continues.

Creating the Strategies

For every objective set, you will create a list of strategies. A strategy, simply defined, is "a particular approach we choose to accomplish the objective." A properly stated strategy will

◆ describe a specific action
◆ have a specific time frame
◆ start with a verb since it is action-oriented

Going back to the previous example, a well-stated strategy to help us accomplish an evangelistic objective might be: *Develop (verb) a communication strategy to market the ministries of the church to people living in the surrounding community (specific action) by February 15, 2008 (time specific)*. Another might be: *Conduct a neighborhood phone campaign to introduce ourselves to the people in our community, hear their spiritual-related needs, and invite those without a church home to an outreach event by March 1, 2008.*

Other strategies to accomplish an outreach objective might involve evaluating the church's worship services and programs in terms of visitor-friendliness, holding a community-friendly event like an outdoor concert, or creating a program to train church members in personal evangelism. What these all have in common is that they are approaches that move the church in the direction of accomplishing its stated objective.

> **Those who are directly involved means those who must perform at least one action in order for the objective and strategies to become reality.**

How many strategies should a church or ministry team set? That will depend upon the number of issues the planning team has identified as critical to the successful accomplishment of the objective. We will discuss this further when we look at the structure of the actual planning session later in the chapter. For now, suffice it to say that through your strategies, you will address the critical issues to the satisfaction of all involved in planning.

You will also widen the circle of those involved in planning to those individuals you identify as having a stake in the process—directly or indirectly. Those who are directly involved means those who must perform at least one action in order for the objective and strategies to become reality. Those who are indirectly involved means those you identify as key influencers—they do not do any work relating to the process, but their support will help or hinder the process along the way.

Defining the Action Steps

You have set an objective for the church or your ministry and created a list of strategies that will move you and your team toward accomplishing your goal. The next step is to define action steps to help you accomplish each strategy. Action steps break each strategy into manageable and measurable tactics. A simple definition of an action step is "specific, tangible actions in which people engage to meet goals." A properly stated action step will be tactical in nature:

◆ Reduce strategies to singular, well-defined events
◆ Identify "who" will do "what," and "when" it will be done
◆ Account for financial, facility, and people resources needed to accomplish the objective

In the previous section, we created a hypothetical strategy: *Develop (verb) a communication strategy to market the ministries of the church to people living in the surrounding community (specific action) by February 15, 2008 (time specific).* Breaking this strategy into bite-sized chunks action steps looks something like this:

Jane Jones (who) will develop a list of all the potential communication media including the pros, cons, and cost (resource needs) of using each one (what) by November 1, 2007 (when). One more might be: *Fred Smith (who) will research and create a written report of the church's community-friendly events for the next 12 months and deliver the report to the team (what) by November 15, 2007 (when).* These tactical steps will move the ministry team in the direction of creating its communication strategy for marketing church ministries to the surrounding community. This, in turn, will help the church achieve its goal of welcoming 100 previously unchurched people to the church family by January 1, 2008.

Once you are working at the level of action steps, the goal begins to "feel" achievable. People coalesce around the cause and are engaged in the process. You have created a means not only for accomplishing the goals of the church, but also for evaluating effectiveness along the way.

Now that you have a working definition of objectives, strategies, and action steps, it's time to move to the work of the actual strategic planning session. The next sections will take you through the stages of preparing for the planning session, creating the agenda for the session itself, and overseeing the post-planning session follow up.

Advance Work—Preparing for a Strategic Planning Session

You will be expending the people resources of your church in order to conduct a strategic planning session. Advance preparation is critical if you want to be a wise steward of people's time and create an environment for efficient collaboration. Strategic planning leads to order, but it also gets messy at certain points. The more clarity you can bring upfront to the process, the better for you and the team in the long run. The following sections capture areas you will need to give attention to in advance of the strategic planning session.

Build the Right Foundation

Your strategic plan should flow from your vision, mission, and values. If you have not already captured these in writing for your church or ministry, you will need to do so first. Chapter 5 takes you through these processes. Vision, mission, and values lay an important foundation for planning. You will want to share the written version of these with the people who will be involved in the strategic planning session, both before and during the meeting.

Get the Right People Involved

Your next step will be to determine who should be invited to participate in the strategic planning session. Make a list of people who would fit into the following categories:

Process facilitator—the person who will lead the strategic planning session. He or she must stay objective and "own" the challenging task of keeping people on track. This individual must also stay true to the process without deviation. Some ministry leaders serve as process facilitators themselves. If you know of someone who is a skilled facilitator, invite him or her to lead the session. The facilitator does not need to be an "insider" with knowledge of the inner workings of the church or ministry. It can be helpful to the objectivity of the process if the facilitator operates outside of the ministry area holding the planning session. Having an outside facilitator is preferred, but not necessary. With advance preparation and careful attention to details, you can serve in this role.

Meeting administrator—the individual charged with ensuring the administrative details of the meeting are handled. Details include note-taking, assigning people who can scribe key points on flip chart paper or a white board, and arranging for meeting handouts and supplies, room set up, and bringing in food and beverages.

Senior leadership—one or more individuals whose approval and buy-in are necessary for the work about to be done. Who this is will depend on the leadership culture of the church. If the strategic planning being done is on behalf of the entire church, you will need to involve the governing body and senior pastor at the very least. If the planning being done is on behalf of one area of ministry within the church, that ministry's most senior leader should be involved. Ask yourself, "Is there anyone whose authority is absolutely critical for this work to go forward?" You will either need this person's official sanction before you get started, or you will need to involve him or her in the process.

Action takers—the people who will be responsible for carrying out the work created by the planning process. If someone will need to contribute his or her time and service in order for the work to get done, send a meeting invitation. For a ministry area planning session, you would invite the staff and key volunteers.

Key influencers—people who may not have any direct responsibility for the work of the strategic plan, but whose cooperation and collaboration would be beneficial. Perhaps there is someone from another ministry area that you foresee working with down the road. (Example: You are conducting a strategic planning session for the evangelism team. You foresee potential changes to worship, so you invite the worship leader.) Influential leaders can positively impact your work by spreading "good gossip" to others who seek their opinions. On the flip side, if they do not understand what you are doing, then when they are sought out by others, they can create roadblocks, often unknowingly, just by not having an opinion. Invite these people to the planning session and be bold in asking for their support. Chances are they will leave excited for your ministry and eager to tell others about it. They will become advocates and goodwill ambassadors.

The number of people you include on the invitation list will be largely determined by the size of your church or ministry area. Any size church can and should engage in strategic planning. The determining factor is not size—it's a choice to become strategic in your efforts to help make the vision and mission a reality. This can be done with as few as six, or as many as fifteen, of the right people around the planning table.

Get the Timing Right

With vision statement and invitation list in hand, your next step is to determine when to hold your planning session. There are three factors to bear in mind when choosing a time. First, you and those you will involve must make this a priority. This means you all will need to carve out the time necessary for the actual planning session and follow-up work. Second, you will need at least six hours for the strategic planning meeting. Third, the entire strategic planning process should be done in a relatively short time frame. That means it should take no more than eight weeks from start to finish.

Trying to juggle everyone's calendar to find the "perfect" meeting time is an impossible task. You, as the leader, will need to be sensible about selecting a time, but you will ultimately need to make that decision and stick with it. Here are a few things to consider:

- ◆ Other church and community calendar events—such as Christmas, Easter, back-to-school.
- ◆ The people on your list—do they have weekday flexibility, or do you need to hold your planning session(s) in the evening or on a weekend?

◆ Are there days and times when people are already accustomed to attending church meetings?

At some point, you will need to set the date and time. If you have done your homework, you should have chosen a time that will work for most on the list. Part of your responsibility also will be to cast the vision for the importance of the planning session. You will need to convince people to fit it into their schedules.

The strategic planning session may be the only time you will have everyone on your invitation list in a room together at the same time. You should plan on meeting for a minimum of six hours, but no more than twelve. One determining factor for setting the number of hours will be the scope of your work. A church-wide planning session involving governance board or committee members, the senior pastor and other clergy, and key staff perhaps will require more time than a session for the education or evangelism teams. If you have never engaged in strategic planning, you will want to be more generous with the time allotted. In subsequent years, the process will become refined and you will be able to manage your time more efficiently.

The planning session can be done in a single meeting, or split into two or three sessions. If you must split the time, you will want to try to hold the meetings on consecutive days or, at the very least, within the same week. Acknowledge the fact that it won't be easy to fit into your calendars, but that it must be a priority. If you draw out the planning time for more than a few days, valuable momentum will be lost. Part of what makes the process work is the focused energy given to it.

Finally, try to wrap up the work of the plan in a short time frame. The planning process, from the date of the first planning meeting to the completion of the written planning document, should take no more than eight weeks. You have asked everyone to make this a priority. If the post-meeting work drags on, someone will lose credibility and the plan will lose momentum.

Create the Right Environment

Selecting a location for your strategic planning session is an important decision. The best choice will be one that is comfortable and distraction-free, yet business-like. You need to hold in tension the need for space that fosters creativity but also has a professional quality. You do not need a fancy conference room—there are things you can do to the space to set the stage for a productive time with the planning group.

Make sure your space is clutter-free. Messy space inhibits free-flow thinking. The room will need to be well-lit and temperature-controlled. A room that is too bright, too dim, too cold, or too hot will make your participants uncomfortable. Don't limit yourself to rooms in the church building. Local libraries and community centers often have meeting spaces. Church retreat sites work well. Or, ask around to see if any church members have offices with conference room space.

Consider the set up of the room. You want people seated at tables facing one another. Setting tables in a large square works well. People need to be able to make eye contact and hear each other when speaking. You will also need an easel with flip chart paper. The flip chart paper gives you the ability to fill many pages and post these around the room. You will see how this is critical to the process a little later in the chapter. Also, the meeting administrator can take the flip chart pages with him or her to aid in capturing notes from the meeting. Either purchase self-sticking easel paper that can be tacked up on the walls, or bring tape that can be safely used on the wall surface. Don't forget to bring markers.

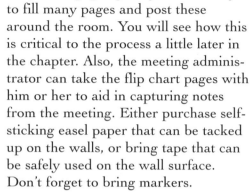

Consider the set up of the room. You want people seated at tables facing one another.

Have your paperwork in order. Be sure there are enough copies of the agenda, along with any other documentation pertinent to the process, such as the vision and mission statements. Consider having blank note pads and pens available for meeting participants.

One last consideration for the comfort of your planning participants will be providing food and beverages. If you are keeping people over a normal eating time, plan to provide a meal. Choose something nice, but simple, that can be eaten while you work. If you meet in the morning, have coffee. If you meet into the evening, your beverage choices should include decaffeinated options. Ask people if they have special concerns relating to food and drink before the meeting. Keep cold water plentiful and handy. Have someone bring healthy snacks. Place small, individually-wrapped mints and candies on the tables. You need to properly care for the people who are giving of their time and service.

Send the Right Message

You have considered the "who," "what," and "where" of the strategic planning process. It's now time to extend the invitations. Before you do, read through the entire chapter and be clear in your own mind about what will happen during the planning meeting. Create a simple agenda that highlights the general steps of the meeting:

◆ Welcome and introductions
◆ Opening devotion and prayer
◆ Ground rules for the planning session

Communicating the vision, mission, and values
Assessing the current situation (present)
Identifying key issues (future)
Setting the objectives
◆ Breating strategies
◆ Developing action steps
Next steps and follow up

At this point, you do not need to set the times for the agenda items, but you do want those invited to get a picture of what they will be doing during the meeting.

You will want to send the written vision, mission, and values document to those you invite to the planning meeting. You will need to provide the general theme of the meeting. For example, "We'll be setting church-wide/ministry area objectives based upon where God is leading our church/ministry in the next two years." Tell the members of the planning group what you envision the group will accomplish. An example: "Together, we'll create the marching orders for our ministry for the next two years."

You also will want to convey three key requirements of the planning session:

◆ It begins with a definite purpose in mind—the vision and mission.
It requires an understanding of the environment in which the church or ministry finds itself; the emphasis will be on issues and obstacles that would impede success.
The group members will engage in a creative approach to respond to those issues and obstacles.

Extend the invitation in writing. Your letter should cast a vision for your time together and include the essential elements of a strategic planning session. Send along the vision, mission, and values statements document and the simple agenda. Your invitation strategy should include personal contact—face-to-face or by telephone. State in the invitation letter that you will follow up personally, or invite the invitees to call you. Be sure to have an RSVP contact and date. As a part of the RSVP, ask that invitees alert you if they have any special dietary concerns. Invite them to be in prayer in the time leading up to the strategic planning session. Now, you are ready for planning day!

Planning Day—A Spirit-filled and Spirit-led Strategy Session

This section of the chapter will serve as a checklist for the meeting facilitator. Strategic planning is a disciplined process, and as such, the facilitator is charged with keeping the meeting focused and productive. It is also messy at times. There will be points during the meeting when participants will become frustrated and the facilitator may be tempted to deviate from the agenda or meeting ground rules. Do not let this happen.

Begin with step one and follow this list in order. The facilitator also serves the group by maintaining the schedule for the session. Guidelines for time are suggested for each step. Build in a fifteen-minute break at least every two hours. Trust the process. It will all make sense in the end.

1. Welcome and introductions (15 minutes)

Do not neglect this basic, simple step. Welcome everyone in attendance and thank them for their participation. Let them know they have been invited because their participation is crucial to the success of the process. Take time to have people introduce themselves, and be sure to provide name tags if there is even one person in the room who does not know everyone else. This can be led by someone other than the facilitator.

2. Opening devotion and prayer (15-30 minutes)

Strategic planning by nature feels very business-like. It should not be so. You are counting on the fact that God will work through each and every individual gathered to speak words of wisdom to the group. Every person is meant to contribute.

Set the stage by having a time of Bible-based devotion and prayer led by a pastor or key leader of the church or ministry. Take into account what feels right for your church culture. If people are accustomed to singing, then, by all means, sing. You are inviting the Holy Spirit to guide the process and speak through those gathered. Do whatever it takes to set a Spirit-filled and Spirit-guided tone in your setting.

You are also inviting God to speak to the group about your church's or your ministry area's unique calling. What is God directing your group to do that will result in growth for the church or its members? How might God want to impact the community through your church or ministry? What is God counting on you to do that will go undone if you do not do it?

3. Ground rules for the planning session (5-10 minutes)

This next item requires a little finesse on the part of the facilitator, yet the facilitator must also be firm. Ask the people gathered for their trust. They will need to trust the facilitator and the process. There will be times during the session when they will engage in open brainstorming. During these times, some will feel tempted to "problem solve." This is not allowed. Period. The goal is to identify issues and potential roadblocks to achieving success. Strategies will flow from these issues. Problems will be solved as action steps are taken as a result of the plan. Engaging in problem-solving during the strategic planning meeting will derail the process. Here, then, are the ground rules:

- Everyone will be given an opportunity to speak and contribute.
- No judgments will be made—no debates allowed.
- Issues should be raised—but not solutions.
- Opportunity areas will be identified—we will not share stories of what has and has not worked in the past.
- The focus will be on process—not on people.
- Strategic planning will become an ongoing component of the ministry area.
- The goal of the day will be to identify and write at least one objective, create written strategies to achieve the objective, and develop at least one full set of action steps for a strategy, also in writing (see the Strategic Planning Templates provided in the Appendix). (Note: We will define objective, strategy, and action step later in this chapter.)
- The objective must be in harmony with the vision, mission, and values of the church.
- People will leave with assignments to finish the written plan if it is not complete at the end of the meeting.
- We will discuss next steps before we leave.

4. Vision, mission, and values of the church and ministry (10-15 minutes)

Take time to walk through the vision, mission, and core values of the church—and ministry, if applicable. If the facilitator is not a ministry leader, it would be a good idea to invite the most senior leader of the ministry for which the plan is being created to lead this section. Doing this contributes to the overall tone of the meeting since you are creating plans to move you in the direction of the vision, help you accomplish the mission, and operate in alignment with your values.

5. Assessing the current situation (15-60 minutes)

The amount of time you spend on this step will depend upon the history of the ministry that is the subject of the strategic plan. Ask someone to capture in bulleted points on flip chart paper the comments from the group. If you are engaged in strategic planning for a brand new ministry, you have no history other than what has led to the decision to create this ministry. If this is the case, have someone who has been intimately involved with that decision present a brief history.

If the strategic planning session is being done on behalf of the church or an established ministry, take time to engage the group in an open discussion of the "current state of the church/ministry." The goal of this step is to capture in writing answers to the following questions:

- What words or phrases would people on the outside use to describe your church/ministry?

◆ In what tangible ways is the church/ministry fulfilling its vision and mission?
◆ What are your strengths?
◆ What's not working?

Sticking with the evangelism team example, some possible responses you'll find on your flip chart might be:
◆ *The church has about 100 first-time visitors each year.*
◆ *Twenty people, most of whom did not have a previous church home, joined the church last year.*
◆ *People in the community say positive things about our children's vacation Bible school.*
◆ *People say our worship service is difficult to follow.*
◆ *We sent out only one direct mailing to the community in the last year.*

This step has the potential of causing some discomfort in the room. The facilitator should explain this in advance and advise people to be factual and brief with their answers. Let people know the goal of this time is to create a word picture of the current state of the ministry.

Perceptions will vary from person to person—that is normal. You are engaging in a process to get those perceptions out in the open and captured on flip chart paper. How they will be dealt with will be a matter discussed later in the agenda. In the meantime, the group will not take time to debate the validity of any one individual's perceptions. All are valid. The facilitator can ask questions if any given response lacks clarity. As the meeting progresses, people will begin to get the "hang of" giving properly stated responses.

Begin to wrap this section up as you near one hour. If you sense there is still productive input to be shared, the facilitator can engage people during the break and share the additional ideas as a lead-in to the next section. Take the flip chart pages with these ideas and hang them on one of the walls. Allow people to mill around them during the breaks and add to them later, but tell the group if something is added. Be sure each page of the flip chart paper has the heading "current situation" written at the top to avoid confusion later.

By now you are likely close to two hours into your meeting. This would be a good time to take a fifteen-minute break.

6. Identifying key issues—envisioning the future (90 minutes)

The purpose of the previous step was to paint a word picture of the current situation in which your church or ministry finds itself. The focus of this next step is the future. This should be led by the facilitator. Take time to remind participants of one of the ground rules—no problem-solving will be allowed.

Often the group will begin to self-police, and someone will shout out "no problem-solving" when the group begins to drift in that direction.

Remind the group of the vision, mission, and values of the church or ministry. Engage in a brainstorming session set up as follows:

"Taking into consideration the vision of the church/ministry (the direction God is leading us), our mission (the reason we exist), and our core values, what are some of the key issues and potential roadblocks we face in living into our potential? In other words, what must we address in order to be all God intends us to be?"

Have one or two scribes ready to capture the issues raised on pages of flip chart paper. Sticking with the evangelism team example, you will begin to generate a list of issues that might look something like this:

> *We need a larger evangelism team.*
> *The church needs to plan community-friendly events.*
> *Worship should be visitor-friendly.*
> *We don't know our community or their needs.*
> *Help is needed to create better direct mail pieces.*
> *We don't have an overall marketing/communication strategy.*
> *We need a bigger budget.*

Your list probably will fill several pages of flip chart paper. Some of your participants, including yourself, may become frustrated because the facilitator will not allow them to problem-solve. The goal of this stage of planning is to get out into the open every possible issue and roadblock related to the ministry. When you do move on to problem-solving, you will all feel more confident that every potential detail was taken into account; and people will have more confidence in the finished product.

Hang the sheets of flip chart paper on a wall opposite the "current situation" sheets. Be sure to label each "key issues." This is a great place for another break—perhaps it is time to serve a meal if you have planned an all-day session. Invite people to review all of the lists and add to them. Begin the next segment of the meeting by updating the group on the additions.

7. Defining the objectives/goals for the future (60-90 minutes)

Take a few moments to celebrate the work the group has already accomplished. It is now time to engage the group in actual planning, which for some may come as a relief. The facilitator will need to define for the group what an objective is, and is not. Here is the definition you were given earlier in the chapter: "the ends we wish to accomplish in a specified time frame." A properly stated objective will

- ◆ clearly state the desired result
- ◆ be measurable and time specific
- ◆ paint a picture of a point in the future
- ◆ be critical to the success of your ministry
- ◆ move you beyond the normal day-to-day operations of the church

Give the participants examples of a properly and improperly stated objective in writing. The examples we used earlier in the chapter are as follows:

By January 1, 2008 (time specific), of the people from our community who were previously without a church home (critical to success), 100 will have become members of our church family (measurable). (properly stated)

People without a church home will join our church. (improperly stated)

The facilitator is asking the group to create one or more objectives, taking into account the vision and mission of the church or ministry. The objective should be something new that goes beyond the scope of day-to-day operations and reaches no more than two years into the future. Ask the group, *"As you look two years into the future of this ministry, what do you envision we will have accomplished?"* Define that "state of being" in one or more sentences and try to develop an objective for each sentence.

The objective, or objectives, will not address all of the key issues. That is the work of the strategies that will be created a little later. Set a limit of one to three objectives. (A church should set five or less.) Balance the need to stretch yourselves to that which is achievable only with God, with the reality of the situation you find yourself in. Here's where the work of the Holy Spirit will be very evident. The group will work through this process together.

Get drafts of properly stated objectives on paper, one objective per sheet of flip chart paper. Assign each objective an "owner." This is the person who will ultimately be accountable for ensuring each objective is met and will bear responsibility for meeting with and holding others accountable for their assigned action steps.

Allow yourselves the freedom to refine the objectives at any point throughout the meeting. Once the group reaches consensus that it has at least a decent draft of one or more objectives, you are ready to move on to creating strategies after a short break.

8. Creating strategies—dealing with key issues (90 minutes)

If you have more than one objective, you will need to assign them sequential numbers starting with one. The next stage of the process is to create a list of strategies that will help you achieve the stated objective. It is time to define for the group what a strategy is, citing examples of properly and improperly stated strategies. Here are the definition and examples from earlier in the chapter: A strategy, simply defined, is "a particular approach we choose to accomplish the objective." A properly stated strategy will:
   ◆ describe a specific action
   ◆ have a specific time frame
   ◆ start with a verb since it is action-oriented

A well-stated strategy to help us accomplish an evangelistic objective might be: *Develop (verb) a communication strategy to market the ministries of the church to people living in the surrounding community (specific action) by February 15, 2008 (time specific)*. Another might be: *Conduct a neighborhood phone campaign to introduce ourselves to the people in our community, hear their spiritual-related needs, and invite those without a church home to an outreach event by March 1, 2008.*

The basis for these strategies will be the lists of key issues the group generated earlier. In essence, by the time you finish the planning process, you should be able to point to someplace within the written plan where it deals with each key issue. Part of the task of both the group and the facilitator will be to group the key issues into categories as you work. For example, you may have identified several issues that deal with communication and marketing. These may become one strategy to develop a comprehensive marketing and communication plan by a set deadline. As you move toward developing the bite-sized tactics under each strategy, you should be able to cross off issues on the list as they are accounted for in the overall plan.

Think of the process as creating buckets. You might have buckets labeled as follows:

◆ Communication and marketing
◆ Staffing and leadership structure
◆ Budget and resources
◆ Community needs assessment
◆ Events planning

These are some of the major categories that seem to envelope most issues and obstacles. As you all work through the process, your own "buckets" will emerge. You may name some and later decide to combine categories. This is a dynamic process. Don't be afraid to make changes at any point during the plan writing stages.

Each strategy you create will be numbered in a way that will tie it back to the particular objective it helps to achieve. If you started with only one objective, number each strategy sequentially, starting with one. If you have two or more objectives, number your strategies sequentially, but start with the number of the objective. For example, if you are working on an objective to which you assigned the number one, your strategies should be numbered 1.1, 1.2, 1.3, 1.4, and so on. There are templates in the Appendix (see pp. 129-132) that you can use to create your final written plan. The owner of the objective will own the strategies, or assign ownership with another's consent.

If you have more than one objective, you have a decision to make. Depending on the time you have allotted for the strategic planning session, you may choose to fully develop only one objective with the group. If this is the case, one of the next steps you will need to take is to assign the development of the entire plan to people at the meeting. Generally, these are people who are key stakeholders in the area being developed. Whatever you decide, you need to allow enough time to take one objective through to the action steps stage. Be encouraged—you are getting close to the finish line. Give the group a well-deserved stretch break and regroup to start developing the action steps.

9. Developing action steps—who, what, and when (60-90 minutes)

As a final step in the process, choose at least one strategy for which you will fully develop action steps. Provide participants with the definition and examples. To review our earlier material, a simple definition of an action step is "specific, tangible actions in which people engage to meet goals." A properly stated action step will

- ◆ be tactical in nature
- ◆ reduce strategies to singular, well-defined events
- ◆ identify "who" will do "what," and "when" it will be done
- ◆ account for financial, facility, and people resources needed to accomplish the objective

We previously created a hypothetical strategy to: *Develop (verb) a communication strategy to market the ministries of the church to people living in the surrounding community (specific action) by February 15, 2007 (time specific).* Breaking down this strategy into bite-sized action steps looks something like this:

Jane Jones (who) will develop a list of all the potential communication media including the pros, cons, and cost (resource needs) of using each one (what) by November 1, 2007 (when). One more might be: *Fred Smith (who) will research and create a written report of the church's community-friendly events for the next twelve months and deliver the report to the team (what) by November 15, 2007 (when).*

In this last step, you take each strategy and break it down into manageable actions. For each action, you determine who will be responsible, when the step will be completed, what resources will be needed to accomplish the task, and what will constitute a measurable, tangible result of the action being taken. These, too, will be numbered sequentially. If you are developing action steps for an objective you've assigned the number 2, under which you have created a strategy numbered 4, you will begin numbering the action steps 2.4.1, 2.4.2, 2.4.3, 2.4.4, and so on. Again, templates are included in the Appendix.

Work as a group to develop as many objectives, strategies, and action steps as time will allow. It is very likely you will need to finish and refine the final written strategic plan after the conclusion of your planning session. This leads us to the final agenda item—next steps.

10. Next steps and follow up (15-30 minutes)

By now, everyone in the room is both exhausted and exhilarated—exhausted because you have all worked very hard; exhilarated because together you have taken a God-sized dream and reduced it to challenging, yet manageable action steps. As each is accomplished, the vision is nearer to becoming reality. The feeling is awesome.

The final step is to assign any work that must be done to complete the written plan. Like any other action step, an owner and deadline will be set. You will need to provide blank templates to those assigned the task and provide them with the notes taken during the meeting. Remember, you chose a meeting administrator to capture the work being done. This individual can take the flip chart sheets and create meeting minutes for use by those completing the written plan.

The final document should be completed no later than eight weeks from the date of the strategic planning session. Set a timetable for its completion. Once finished, it should be distributed to everyone who attended.

Thank everyone in attendance. Pause to thank God in prayer and to ask for continued guidance as you fulfill the work that has begun. "High fives" would not be out of line at this point!

Post-Planning Day—Building in Accountability, Next Steps, and Follow Up

What happens after the strategic planning session is as important as the preparation and the session itself. The ministry leader will ultimately be responsible for the successful execution of the final strategic plan. Here is a checklist of items to be considered:

◆ Distribute the finished plan to everyone who participated in the planning session.

◆ Secure the resources necessary for the accomplishment of the plan. Action steps may require funding, the use of church facilities, or a host of other resource-related issues.

◆ Set meetings with action step owners for the purpose of reporting progress at least bi-monthly. Deadlines that were created need to be met. It is also possible the plan will need to be refined along the way. You may engage in something relating to a strategy and find it is not the right step. Remember, the plan is also dynamic and fluid. Meetings with action step owners should also serve as occasions for celebration, encouragement, and prayer.

◆ Gather your original group, plus any new leaders or team members, in one year to revisit the plan and potentially engage in the creation of a new one.

In each subsequent year, you will find the process becoming more familiar and easier to facilitate. After a few years, you will have helped to create a culture where strategic planning has become integral to the life of the church.

Reaping the Rewards of Strategic Planning

If you have never engaged in formal strategic planning, you might find the content of this chapter a little overwhelming. Strategic planning is a skill that can be learned. It does seem awkward at first, but with practice the skill is honed. Once honed, strategic planning becomes one of the most useful tools in a leader's toolbox. When first getting started, it is tempting to shortcut the process. Resist the urge. As your strategic skills develop, the process will become easier.

If you need a source of motivation, keep these benefits in mind:

◆ Strategic planning is a proven process—executed properly, it really works.
◆ God-sized visions can seem unattainable. Strategic plans not only break down the vision into manageable pieces; they also serve to distribute the workload as greater numbers of people become involved.
◆ Planning sessions have a unifying effect—as people work through issues and create strategies, they collaborate and coalesce in support of the work of the church.
◆ We honor God when we give the work of the church our very best efforts.

And, the last word from Scripture—

This is the plan that is planned concerning the whole earth; and this is the hand that is stretched out over all the nations. For the LORD of hosts has planned, and who will annul it? His hand is stretched out, and who will turn it back? (Isaiah 14:26, 27)

Questions for Reflection or Discussion

1. Why is the ability to effectively conduct strategic planning such an important skill for a leader?

2. Have you ever had an experience when a really great idea or vision never got off the ground? Describe what happened. What could have been done differently that might have helped the idea come to fruition?

3. What do you think will be your greatest obstacle to successful strategic planning? How will you overcome this obstacle?

4. Describe a personal dream or vision you have for the future. How might you utilize the strategic planning process to help make your dream a reality? List a few concrete steps you can take right now to achieve your vision.

CHAPTER 7

Effective Communication

*"My words come from an upright heart;
my lips sincerely speak what I know." (Job 33:3)*

The phrase "effective communication" is sometimes perceived as an over-used business "buzzword," but we only have to experience ineffective communication once or twice to understand just how important clear communication really is. We've all played the children's game "telephone" at one time or another where you start with a message that is passed from person to person in a line. Almost without exception, the message that is repeated aloud by the last person in line is different from the original.

Even when we think we're communicating clearly, sometimes signals get crossed. What we say is not always what the listener hears. Occasionally, the message is heard correctly, but the intent is misinterpreted.

When my (Yvonne's) daughter was a teenager, we had countless conversations (well, I thought they were conversations; she thought they were lectures) during which she would say, "Stop yelling at me!" Invariably my voice wasn't raised, nor was I angry; and I would deny that I was yelling. As you can imagine, we would end up arguing about whether or not I was yelling, so that the original topic was completely forgotten. How does that happen?

Communication only partially occurs through the words we speak. In fact, our actual words constitute a very small part of the message that is received. Our message is "heard" through our words, our tone, and our body language.

In this broader sense, communication can be defined as "the exchange of thoughts, messages, or information through words, tone, or behavior." My daughter was responding to the tone of my voice and the expression on my face more than to the words I was speaking. Whether I was aware of it or not, I was communicating anger. This type of miscommunication doesn't just happen at home; it takes place in the office, at church, and elsewhere.

Consider the various ways the phrase "Way to go!" might be interpreted. Given each stated meaning, identify the tone and body language that might be used:

Case 1: Sincere congratulations
Tone:
Body language:

Case 2: Teasing someone about a mistake or misstep
Tone:
Body language:

Case 3: Frustration or anger
Tone:
Body language:

Communication is, by definition, an "exchange" composed of both the message sent and the message received. Those two parts must match in order for the communication to be effective. Effective communication is critical to building effective relationships, teams, and ministries. If it's so important, why do we do it so poorly? Primarily because we are often moving so fast that we communicate without taking the time to consider carefully how we can best achieve our communication goals and then act accordingly.

Barriers to Effective Communication

The vast majority of the problems that surround communication arise from three issues:
1. Lack of message clarity
2. Poor listening skills
3. Improper mode of communication/Poor use of communication

1. Lack of Message Clarity

A few years ago, I was partnering with three other people to facilitate a Christian leadership class. One person was the program leader, who would attend every session, and the rest of us would alternate serving as class facilitator. The four of us met for breakfast one day to organize our class format and lesson plans, and to determine the critical "take-aways" for each session. We left the restaurant with complete agreement (or so we thought) about what our approach would be.

A few weeks later, I received a call from the program leader. She felt one member of the team was off-track, and she asked me to intervene. I sent an email to the entire four-person team, restating the major points we had agreed to at our meeting as a way of making sure we were on the same page. I received confirmation from one person. From the other, I received a confirmation email that said, "What I hear you saying is that I need to do ____," which was completely different from what I had put in the email. I thought I had been clear, but obviously the message received was not the message I believed I had sent.

I placed a follow-up phone call to this individual, explaining that there was some misunderstanding, and going point-by-point over what we needed. Again, I thought we were in sync. A few weeks later, I received another call from the program leader who said that things had not improved. This time I decided we needed a face-to-face meeting. I was concerned because I felt that I had clearly said what I needed to say, and I wasn't sure how else to communicate the message.

As we talked, I asked a lot of questions and sought feedback on each element of the discussion. I began to understand that the underlying issue was not a misunderstanding of the class format or lesson plan but a misunderstanding of the priorities of the program itself, which caused the gaps in expectations versus execution. Once we achieved clarity on that point, we were able to get in tune.

What I learned is that even if my message is clear, the perspective of the person I am communicating to will color how he or she interprets what I am saying. I could have talked until I was blue in the face and still would have gotten nowhere. What I needed to do was ask questions and listen!

Achieving Clarity of Message

Excellent communication doesn't happen by accident. People who communicate with great clarity are very intentional about how they frame and send their messages. Using these three fundamentals of clear communication will help you get your message across more effectively:

Purpose

> What's the point of your communication? Are you hoping to inspire, to encourage, or simply to pass along information? Is some action required on the part of the person(s) receiving your message? Your primary goal will shape the outline of your message, the mode of communication you should use, and the tone you'll take. We'll talk in more detail about these various types of communication later in the chapter.

Perspective

> Carefully consider the perspective of your audience. If you are addressing a group, do they share a common frame of reference that you need to bear in mind? Are there preconceived notions you need to address? What obstacles or objections to your message might you need to overcome? Is there something in the audience's background that will resonate with your message? If not, how can you make your message engaging? If you are addressing an individual, does he or she have a preferred mode of communication?

Plain language

> Joseph Priestly, an eighteenth-century chemist and clergyman, said it well: "The more elaborate our…communication, the less we communicate." The best communication is simple and concise. Don't try to

impress people with your broad vocabulary. Keep your language plain by using short words—and as few of them as necessary to deliver your meaning.

2. Poor Listening Skills

Many of us are like the servant in Isaiah 42:20: "He sees many things, but does not observe them; his ears are open, but he does not hear." We are poor listeners. We may have good intentions, but sometimes there are barriers to effective listening. These include:

- ◆ Lack of awareness. We're too preoccupied with our own thoughts and problems to pay attention to someone else's.
- ◆ Avoiding. We're aware of the message, but we don't want to hear it.
- ◆ Assuming. We think we "know" what's going to be said.
- ◆ Confronting. We're busy formulating our response to what's being said.
- ◆ Perception. How the message is delivered is an impediment to our "hearing" it.

You've probably heard of the concept of "active listening," where the listener reflects back to the speaker his or her understanding of what is being said. I'd like to encourage you to go one step further and practice "dynamic listening." Dynamic listening requires not only your attention but also your full participation.

Dynamic listening uses the Socratic method of gaining insight: pretending ignorance and asking a lot of questions. It involves seeking more information ("Tell me more about that…") and confirming understanding repeatedly ("What I hear you saying is…"). For example, if Janet and David were discussing their thoughts on careers/hard work, and Janet expressed that she valued her career and earning more money over having leisure time, which David preferred, David might just walk away thinking that Janet was a workaholic and completely inconsiderate of her family's needs. Through dynamic listening, though, David might gain a different perspective. Imagine the following conversation:

Janet: "It's really important to me to earn a lot of money. I want to be able to provide my family with what they need."

David: "But I think spending time with your family is much more important than giving them 'things.' Why is earning money so important? Couldn't you make do with less?"

Janet: "We could, and I have. When I was growing up, my family was very poor. All my clothes were either hand-me-downs or homemade. I felt like a second-class citizen. We sometimes went without things that most people consider necessities. I don't want my kids to experience that."

David: "It sounds like you're worried that it could happen to you again at anytime, and you're trying to protect your family by building a big nest-egg just in case. Do you feel insecure about your job or earning potential for some reason?"

Janet: "That's right. I work on straight commission, and so if I don't work hard, I don't earn anything. Sometimes even when I work really hard, things are just slow and the money doesn't come in. I start to get those same feelings of insecurity again. It's kind of scary!"

David: "Wow. I can see how that would make you feel. I still think your family would rather have more time with you, but I understand your perspective."

Just by asking a couple of questions instead of making assumptions, David has a better understanding of Janet. She feels "heard," and they can agree to disagree without arguing their points. Dynamic listening repeatedly seeks information and confirms understanding while giving full attention to the speaker—without interruption or personal judgments. Dynamic listening helps you hear and understand both what is said and what is felt—the heart of communication.

3. Improper Mode of Communication/Poor Use of Communication

Have you ever said something to someone and immediately realized that the words didn't come out the way you intended? You wish you could hit "rewind" and try to phrase it better the next time. Choosing the wrong mode of communication, or using the right one in an ineffective manner, can have the same results.

Not too long ago, I was leading a team that was redirected toward a new focus, and along with our new focus came a new "boss"—our staff advisor. This individual had a vision for how the new direction would be implemented which was completely different from the vision the existing team had. Almost all the communication received from our advisor was via email.

The team, comprised of a group of subject matter experts, was beginning to feel stifled and discouraged that its ideas were not being given consideration. I felt it was my responsibility as the leader to express the team's concerns. In return, I received an email response that felt like a fiery blast, both in terms of tone and content.

This prompted an equally argumentative (and even longer) email retort from me. The situation was quickly deteriorating. I had team members threatening to resign, I was frustrated, and the new boss wasn't exactly having fun either. He called in reinforcements.

The new contact took a different approach—she picked up the phone and called me. We spent nearly an hour on that call, during which she let me vent my (and the team's) frustrations as she listened carefully, asking questions for clarification. Then she asked for a face-to-face meeting with the team.

At this meeting, the group reached a compromise of sorts. The team came to understand that the vision set by our staff advisor was the vision we would be following, but we were given control for how to implement it. We were able to work together to get the project launched.

Now, don't get me wrong; I love email. It is my preferred mode of communication—it's fast, convenient, and effective for many kinds of communications. However, it is not a good mode of communication when there is any sort of conflict involved. It's difficult if not impossible to interpret someone's tone and intent in email, and this can potentially lead to a serious misunderstanding and hurt feelings.

> **It's difficult if not impossible to interpret someone's tone and intent in email, and this can potentially lead to a serious misunderstanding and hurt feelings.**

I wish I could tell you that everything was back to normal between the members of the team and the staff advisor, but that's not the case. Harsh words and/or actions can be forgiven (and they have been), but they can be very difficult to completely forget. I regret not picking up the phone to call the staff advisor instead of firing off my reactionary response to his email. I also wonder if I would have reacted differently if he'd called me instead of sending the first email. If I had taken a few minutes to consider the most effective means of communicating during this whole episode, and then had followed through on that, it might have made a huge difference in the final outcome.

Selecting and Effectively Using the Right Mode of Communication

Choosing the best mode of communication—written, phone, face-to-face, or other—is the first step in communicating effectively and being understood. This choice depends on your audience and your message. Using the chosen mode of communication to its maximum effectiveness requires a little thought and preparation on your part, which will help you to achieve your goals.

Choosing Your Vehicle

When selecting the mode of communication—your "vehicle" so to speak—consider first your audience:

- How many people are involved? If it's a significant number (only you can decide what is "significant"), determine whether you can appropriately and effectively deliver your message in a group setting. For instance, it isn't practical to call a group meeting just to inform the attendees of another upcoming meeting! For that kind of message, email is probably the best choice.

- If you're communicating with an individual or a limited number of people, what is their preferred mode of communication? If you don't know what a person's communication preferences are, consider how he or she typically communicates to you. If she regularly comes to your office when she could send an email or call, that's a signal that she prefers face-to-face communication. If he responds quickly to emails but is slower to return phone calls, he probably prefers email. If you're not sure, ask! For some people, it's not simply a matter of preference but a matter of practicality. I have one friend who doesn't have access to personal email at work. If I want to have lunch with this friend today, I need to pick up the phone and call.

Then consider the message itself:

- What is the purpose of the communication? If you need to address a serious issue or a problem with someone's attitude or performance, a one-on-one meeting in person is the only option. If the goal is to praise a team's performance or an individual's accomplishments, written communication, whether via email or a greeting card, is perfectly acceptable.

- What is the sensitivity of the communication? If the message is highly sensitive in terms of confidentiality or personal implications, email or any form of written communication is never appropriate. It's too easy for an email to accidentally be sent to the wrong address, or for the wrong person to open the mail, making the communication itself a problem.

- How urgent is the communication? If there is an emergency situation or critical information you need to convey, you can't assume people will pick up their email (we don't all sit in front of our computers all day long). Telephone may be the optimal mode of communicating. For instance, when a member of our group was in a serious accident and was sent by ambulance to the hospital, his wife made one phone call—and that person made one phone call, and that person made one phone call, and so on. Within thirty minutes this couple was surrounded by a support network of prayer warriors and persons ready to give practical assistance.

Using Your Vehicle Effectively

Face-to-Face

When planning a face-to-face communication, the optimal setting depends upon the purpose and desired outcome of your message. We'll discuss how to effectively communicate for different purposes later in the chapter. For now, know that the purpose of the communication will be a key factor in selecting a location for your meeting. For instance, if you are having a celebration dinner for a ministry team, an energetic, noisy restaurant may be appropriate. If the meeting is informational in nature and you need to make sure that everyone understands you, you'll need a quieter setting so that you can be clearly heard.

Tone and body language become even more important to your message when you're communicating face-to-face. You'll need to plan carefully how to most effectively use tone and body language to enhance, rather than distract from, your message.

E-mail and other Written Communications

When email first came on the scene, I loved it for its efficiency. It was fast and usually brief. Now I am inundated with email. It's not unusual for me to receive fifty email messages a day. Unnecessary junk mail comes through with the same degree of importance as vital communication. It takes me as much time to sort through it all as it does to respond. Your experience is probably not much different.

Email is supposed to be efficient. It is best for short, concise communication. If you send a long email message, you should expect that fully half of the recipients will open it, see how long it is, and close it "until they have time to read it," which will likely never happen. If you must send an extensive email communication, put the major points in a summary at the beginning, with all the details following at the end. Always include at the beginning of the email any instructions for action that you need someone to take.

Don't send or reply quickly to emails when emotions are high. Trust me, if you ignore this tip, at some point you'll do something you regret. As it says in Proverbs 29:20, "Do you see someone who is hasty in speech? There is more hope for a fool than for anyone like that."

Use proper grammar and punctuation. USING ALL CAPITAL LETTERS MAKES IT SEEM LIKE YOU'RE YELLING. Using acronyms is equally annoying—in fact, IHA. IDK Y people use them. (That means: I hate acronyms. I don't know why people use them.)

Limit your "forwards" and emoticon usage. Some people I love dearly forward me all kinds of jokes, beautiful inspirational messages, and simple notes with bouncing smiley faces. As much as I'd love to, I can't take the time to read them. They become "junk" mail. If you are leading a team and communicating with the members, you want to be taken seriously. Communicate seriously. That doesn't mean you can't show your personality or have fun with email; just don't make frivolous or silly communication a habit.

For any regular written form of communication, especially one that is distributed to a group of people, using a consistent format can be a helpful tool. A template that provides the essentials first, preferably in bullet points, with details at the end will satisfy those people who want "just the facts" as well as those who want to know all the specifics. Include a clue in the headline as to the type of communication so that people understand the purpose of the communication and how or if they need to respond. A simple header might look like this:

◆ Communication Type: (For instance: *"informational"* or *"action"*)
◆ Action Required: (For instance: *"respond to _____"* or *"none"*)
◆ Due Date:

> # Carefully consider how you communicate meaning and emotions through tone.

There are times when old-fashioned hardcopy or handwritten communications are best. For instance, sending a note of congratulations, sympathy, or thanks should always be written by hand. It is simply more personal and authentic than a note banged out on a keyboard.

Longer documents, memos, policies, and so forth, although typically typed, are most often printed and handed out, mailed, or attached to a shorter email message. Organizing your document with headers and/or bullet points can make it more readable as well as make it easier for recipients to find the critical information they need.

A general rule of thumb is to clearly communicate the main points of the document, including any action required by the recipient, and fill in the details below. If you are mailing the document and require a response, indicate that on the envelope.

Telephone

Tone of voice takes on added importance when communicating via telephone. The person on the other end of the line can't see your facial expressions or read your body language, so he or she will interpret your message primarily based on your tone. Carefully consider how you communicate meaning and emotions through tone. Silence also speaks volumes, and you can use it to communicate certain things such as indecision, disagreement, and so forth. Listen for silence on the other end, too. It's sending a message to you!

Don't use the telephone to communicate when emotions are high, specifically negative emotions. It's too easy to say things that cannot be unsaid.

Remember the words in James 1:19-20, "You must understand this, my beloved: let everyone be quick to listen, slow to speak, and slow to anger; for your anger does not produce God's righteousness." Wait an hour or two (or a day, if necessary) until you can communicate with objectivity. It's not a good practice to leave emotionally charged or confidential messages of any type on an answering machine or voice mailbox, even if you think it's a private one.

Communication Goals

Not long ago, I received a note from a manager in my department highlighting some issues we were facing on a project. It went something like this:

> We have a problem with the XYZ project. The manufacturer isn't responding the way I think he should, and we may miss critical deadlines because of this. I don't think he understands the urgency of the matter. We also are having some communication issues with the _____ department and they have told me they can't provide the support materials we need.

My question to the manager was, "Are you just keeping me informed while you handle this, or do you need me to get involved to help resolve this problem?" She wanted my assistance, but she had not clearly communicated that in her note.

At a company meeting, the CEO was speaking to top management about the company's poor performance. Her facial expression was serious, and her message about the industry forecasts was grim. She told the management team that if something didn't work to turn the business around, things would have to change. How do you think the management group felt as they filed out of the room?

Now imagine that same CEO taking a different approach, telling the group that the situation was serious while also pointing out the positives working in the company's favor and affirming her confidence in the team's ability to turn things around. Do you think the managers might have felt differently leaving that meeting?

It is important to consider your goals in communicating as you prepare your message, both in terms of content and delivery. Spending a little time asking yourself three questions will help you achieve your communication goals:

◆ What is the purpose of this communication?
◆ What response do I want (what do I want people to do or feel)?
◆ How will I trigger that response?

Let's look at the three most common reasons we communicate—to inform, to inspire, and to initiate action—and consider some tips for doing each one more effectively.

Communicating to Inform

In her book *Teach Your Team to Fish*, Laurie Beth Jones tells the story of Barr-Nunn Transportation, which reduced its employee turnover from 55 percent to 35 percent simply by generating a company newsletter that shared interesting and/or important information with everyone in the organization. The employees said the difference was they now felt "connected" (Crown Books, 2002, p. 129).

I'm a big believer in sharing information. I have known some leaders who tend to hoard information, whether intentionally or not, because they feel that knowledge is power. I think this is a critical error in leadership. Your goal in leading is to provide direction and satisfaction to the people who will get things done. Sharing information makes others feel included and engaged in the organization, putting them in position to make better decisions and work more effectively.

> **Your goal in leading is to provide direction and satisfaction to the people who will get things done.**

As you think about passing along information, think carefully about who should be included (I encourage you to be as inclusive as possible) and how much information you can share (share as much as you can, as succinctly as you can). Make sure you include the essentials: who, what, when, where, and why. As mentioned previously, following a template with the vital points at the top and the details following will help you get just the right amount of information to everyone in your audience.

Communicating to Inspire

Whether your goal is to motivate a group toward a shared vision, to rally the team behind an important project, or to encourage someone to take on a new leadership role, communicating a message with the purpose of inspiration requires careful planning. You might want to map out your approach in writing and practice your delivery a few times to feel comfortable with it. You don't want to seem "rehearsed," but you do want to be well-prepared. Keep the following tips in mind:

◆ Be animated. Use passion, emotion, and activity to help convey the message and create excitement.

◆ Use vivid language—stories, metaphors, images, and the senses—to make your message come to life.

◆ Use examples the audience can relate to—you want them to be able to see themselves in the story. In a rural community, a farming example makes perfect sense, but this is probably not the best choice for an audience in the urban core.

◆ Use repetition. Restate your message in different ways. Marketing research shows that consumers must see or hear about a product six to ten times before they'll make a purchase.

◆ Be upbeat and positive. Make the goal seem achievable. Your role as leader is to generate hope and aspiration.

◆ Exude personal conviction. Napoleon Hill, author of *Think and Grow Rich*, said, "Whatever the mind of man can conceive and believe, it can achieve" (Ballentine Books, 1987, p. 14). As a leader, the power of your personal confidence in the achievability of the goal is immeasurable.

◆ Since communicating to inspire is such an important part of leadership, and sometimes is the most difficult type of communication to deliver, we've included a worksheet in the Appendix (p. 133) to help you plan your next inspiring message.

Communicating to Initiate Action

When the goal is to initiate action, the most important thing is to explicitly communicate the need for action—and to do it early. Include the critical information of who, what, and by when. Many times people don't take the actions needed because they don't read far enough into the communication to know that they actually need to *do* something. Sometimes when we communicate verbally we do not plainly state that action is required or set a deadline for when the action must be completed. If communicating via email, consider putting the words "action required" in the subject line.

It's important to make it easy for others to respond. In today's busy world, making it complicated to take action almost ensures that no action will occur. Clearly communicate the purpose for the action. Some people need to know *why* we want them to take action, and they will do so more promptly if they understand the purpose and/or goal of the action.

Getting Your Message Across

By this point, you understand that effective communication is carefully planned, taking into consideration both the audience and the purpose of the message. The message we send is more than our words; it is carried even more in our tone and body language. The largest barriers to communication include lack of clarity, poor listening skills, and choosing the improper mode of communication—or not using it effectively. With some intentionality of effort and a little practice, we can all improve our ability to communicate effectively. Try using the tips included in this chapter to plan your next communication. Your message will come across loud and clear!

Questions for Reflection or Discussion

1. Why is the ability to communicate effectively such an important skill for a leader?

2. What are your biggest barriers to communicating effectively? How can you overcome or compensate for them?

3. What is your preferred mode of communication? How has that bias affected your communication?

4. Describe a time when your message was misunderstood. What might you do differently to achieve a better result?

Managing Conflict

"If it is possible, so far as it depends on you, live peaceably with all."
(Romans 12:18)

The church is a group of loving Christians, all worshiping, living, and serving together in perfect harmony—just as we're instructed in the passage above, right? Well, not exactly. From the days of Adam and Eve, conflict has been part of human life. Conflict is inevitable whenever people are together. Some of Paul's most treasured epistles in the New Testament were written to address conflicts taking place in various local congregations.

Our perceptions of conflict vary based on our experiences. Take a moment now and write down words or phrases that you associate with conflict. These might include feelings, actions, or outcomes.

Now review the words you've written and classify them as positive, negative, or neutral. Note here how many fall into each category:

Positive:
Negative:
Neutral:

My (Yvonne's) guess is that most of the words or phrases you associated with conflict would be classified as negative. Most of us aren't comfortable with conflict. We see it as something that should be avoided, especially in the church. But the truth is that the church is not a conflict-free zone, and quite frankly, it shouldn't be. In his book *The Safest Place on Earth*, Larry Crabb writes, "The difference between spiritual and unspiritual community is not whether conflict exists, but is rather in our attitude toward it and approach to handling it" (Word Publishing, 1999, p. 40). When conflict is managed properly, it can be healthy and even beneficial. Unfortunately, if it isn't managed appropriately, conflict can destroy friendships, ministry teams, or even an entire congregation.

While most of us would prefer to avoid conflict, those of us in leadership roles do not have a choice in the matter. We must take the lead in conflict situations, managing those conflicts in Christ-like ways as we strive to reach positive outcomes for all involved. Our focus in this chapter is to gain understanding of the types of conflict that typically occur, methods for preventing unnecessary and unproductive conflict, and steps to address and manage conflict productively.

Understanding Conflict

What is *conflict?* The first definition that comes to mind is "a state of opposition" or "to engage in a battle or warfare." For our purposes, we'll define conflict as "a state of disharmony between incompatible persons, ideas, or interests." Notice that the conflict doesn't have to be an all-out war or even a battle. If we think about it in terms of being "a state of disharmony," conflict doesn't seem quite so intimidating or destructive.

In fact, as previously stated, this "disharmony" can even be beneficial, leading to a better outcome than would have been reached without the conflict. Let me give you an example.

A few years ago, I (Yvonne) was coaching the ministry team responsible for our church's leadership development program. This team was very effective and was providing foundational training in Christian leadership to over one hundred new and emerging leaders each year through a class offered on Monday evenings. The program used guest presenters (a clergy member or other subject matter expert) and a small group discussion each week.

We began to receive some feedback requesting that we offer the program on a another evening of the week as well, and the team's leadership was divided about whether or not to do so. The leaders were vocal and passionate about their positions. On the one hand, part of the group wanted to make the program accessible to more people. On the other hand, another part of the group was concerned about the ability to effectively "staff" the program with enough volunteers on another evening. Most of the ministry team members and our guest presenters were available on Mondays but not throughout the week. We could recruit and train more ministry team members, but what would we do about the guest presenters?

Someone suggested we could videotape the presenters. This produced more conflicting opinions, equally as passionate. One of the features of the program most appreciated by our participants was the ability to ask questions and interact with the various presenters in an informal setting. We met several times to discuss the situation, and in the end we reached a solution that none of us had even dreamed of prior to the original conflict: *Leadership from the Heart: Learning to Lead with Love and Skill*, a published resource complete with DVD presentations by our guest presenters. This curriculum includes all of the study material used in the program and is now available for any small group to use whenever they like. We also continue to use live, in-person guest presenters in our church on Monday evenings.

Conflict is not something that should be avoided; instead, it should be appropriately addressed and managed. By effectively using conflict management techniques in this situation, the team worked through the conflict, achieving a completely unforeseen outcome that benefited not only those involved but also other congregations that are now able to use our curriculum. Conflict management involves using skills to proactively address conflicts in order to reduce unproductive or destructive results and achieve positive, productive outcomes.

Conflicts usually can be categorized in one of two ways: interpersonal conflicts between two people ("I don't like something you said or did") and situational conflicts ("I don't like the direction we're taking"). Each of these involves different emotions and requires different approaches to manage the conflict and reach resolution.

Managing Conflict

In ministry teams, both interpersonal and situational conflicts can occur, though situational conflicts happen with greater frequency. Interpersonal conflicts are often the result of miscommunication or a misunderstanding, while situational conflicts typically result from real differences of opinion. Both types have the potential to be beneficial if managed appropriately, and both can damage relationships and more if mishandled or ignored.

Interpersonal Conflicts

Conflicts between two persons are often highly emotional, involving a perceived personal attack or offense of some kind. Our feelings are hurt, our ego is bruised, or our sensitivities are disrespected. Typically this type of conflict is an escalation of something much less personal and is the result of a misunderstanding or miscommunication. Left unaddressed, this type of conflict will fester and can be incredibly destructive.

As leaders, we must set the stage for the prevention and/or resolution of this type of conflict. One of the best methods

> **Conflict is not something that should be avoided; instead, it should be appropriately addressed and managed.**

of preventing the escalation of conflict on ministry teams is the adoption of a group covenant (see p. 123 in the Appendix for an outline to help you develop a group covenant). A group covenant explicitly states the expectations for how group members will communicate, interact with one another, and address conflict. Understand, though, that a group covenant won't entirely prevent conflict from occurring. What it will do is help prevent conflict from escalating, because it gives you, as the leader, a tool to use to encourage the persons involved to address the conflict.

Jesus' teaching is quite clear on how we are to manage interpersonal conflicts—honestly and directly, with humility, grace, and love. In the Book of Matthew, Jesus addresses both situations—those in which we have wronged another, and those in which we have been wronged:

"So when you are offering your gift at the altar, if you remember that your brother or sister has something against you, leave your gift there before the altar and go; first be reconciled to your brother or sister, and then come and offer your gift." (Matthew 5:23-24)

"If another member of the church sins against you, go and point out the fault when the two of you are alone. If the member listens to you, you have regained that one." (Matthew 18:15)

Notice that in both situations—whether we have done wrong or feel we have been wronged—Jesus' instruction is the same: We are to seek out the other person and address the situation face-to-face, and we are to do it quickly. Jesus does not leave the door open for letting the situation fester or escalate. At the same time, he does not endorse talking to other people about the situation until we have talked directly to the person involved. In other words, we have to take active responsibility for addressing the conflict—regardless of whether we started it or not. Only after doing so is it acceptable to bring another person (a pastor or another person to serve as mediator) into the conflict, and only then for the purpose of mediation and reaching resolution.

> # If at all possible, you should address a conflict within twenty-four hours of becoming aware of its existence.

We recommend using the twenty-four-hour rule, which simply states that if at all possible, you should address a conflict within twenty-four hours of becoming aware of its existence. The meeting should take place face-to-face. It is usually not a good idea to address personal conflicts via email or telephone. These methods of communication have too much potential for further misunderstanding. If you can't meet within twenty-four hours, make contact within twenty-four hours in order to arrange a meeting time and place.

As leaders, we are responsible for setting the expectation that conflicts will be handled in this way. This means that when a team member comes to us with complaints about another, we direct their attention to these scripture passages and our team covenant, and we encourage that person to go directly to the other party. We might offer some coaching, reminding the team member to be specific about what the issue is (that is, "Here is what happened, and this is how it made me feel") and what outcome he or she desires, while maintaining an attitude of respect and grace.

For instance, in a situation where I have done wrong, my approach might be: "Amy, I want to apologize. Last week I said _____, and later I realized that it might have hurt your feelings. That wasn't my intention, and I have regretted my words. I'm truly sorry, and I hope you'll forgive me." Humility, love, and directness are the underlying attitudes here.

If I feel I've been wronged, my approach might be something like this: "Amy, last week you said (or did) _____. Your words (or actions) bothered me because _____. I can't just let it go, because our relationship is too important to me. Maybe you weren't even aware of that situation or how your words sounded (or actions appeared), but now that you do, I would really appreciate it if you wouldn't say (or do) that again." In this case, honesty, love, and grace are the underlying attitudes.

While Jesus expected conflict to occur, he always instructed his followers to treat one another with love. Paul repeated that expectation in Colossians 3:12-15:

> As God's chosen ones, holy and beloved, clothe yourselves with compassion, kindness, humility, meekness, and patience. Bear with one another and, if anyone has a complaint against another, forgive each other; just as the Lord has forgiven you, so you also must forgive. Above all, clothe yourselves with love, which binds everything together in perfect harmony. And let the peace of Christ rule in your hearts, to which indeed you were called in the one body.

Our role as leaders includes holding our group members accountable to these same expectations. When interpersonal conflicts are addressed directly with humility, love, and grace, they can lead to a deeper understanding and appreciation for each other, resulting in stronger bonds and more productive working relationships.

As team leader, you may be the person called in to mediate a conflict on your ministry team. Even if you are not asked to mediate, if you know that a conflict is escalating between members of your team, you will need to step in to help them resolve the problem. You should carefully think through and prepare for the meeting in advance. Consider your desired outcomes, the causes, the responses you might receive, and how you will approach the discussion. To help you work through this, we've included a tool for planning a conflict resolution session in the Appendix (p. 135).

Some people, however, will struggle with working through conflict. We've all known someone who would rather talk about the other person to ten people who are not even involved in the conflict than to talk directly to the other person involved in the "state of disharmony." As a leader, we cannot permit an unwillingness to address conflict directly to poison the entire team, leading to bitterness, resentment, and even separation from the church. This means that at some point we may be in a situation that requires us to ask someone to leave the group if he or she cannot live up to the group covenant's conflict management expectations. This is never a pleasant situation, but it is occasionally—though, thankfully, infrequently—necessary.

Situational Conflicts

Most conflicts in ministry settings are situational in nature. In other words, the conflicts are not personal; they are related to differences of opinion regarding what actions to take, which direction to move in, or what the priorities should be. While the people involved in this type of conflict can be passionate about their positions, situational conflicts are less likely to become personal. When managed appropriately, situational conflicts frequently lead to positive, beneficial outcomes, with all parties feeling respected, valued, and included in the process.

> **As a leader, you can create an environment that encourages healthy, productive conflict.**

As a leader, you can create an environment that encourages healthy, productive conflict. In fact, you want some conflict to occur. If you lead a team that never voices differing opinions, you have a team trapped in "group think," where everyone just goes along with the first idea presented. That means the group probably never reaches its maximum potential. When you set the stage for open, respectful dialogue and the honest sharing of ideas, you develop a group with the potential for synergistic energy, which develops optimum results. (As we discussed in chapter 3, synergy is the interaction of two or more agents or forces so that their combined effect is greater than the sum of their individual effects.)

So how do you do this? First, set the expectations for how the group will work together. We recommend two clearly stated rules that all team members must agree to uphold:

◆ Idea-sharing, questioning the status-quo, and open dialogue is encouraged within the group. We will not discuss or denigrate another person's ideas outside the group.

◆ Disagreement about ideas and direction is expected, but personal attacks or put-downs will not be tolerated.

Remind team members to debate ideas but to respect and build one another up:

> Let no evil talk come out of your mouths, but only what is useful for building up, as there is need, so that your words may give grace to those who hear. And do not grieve the Holy Spirit of God, with which you were marked with a seal for the day of redemption. Put away from you all bitterness and wrath and anger and wrangling and slander, together with all malice, and be kind to one another, tender-hearted, forgiving one another, as God in Christ has forgiven you. Therefore be imitators of God, as beloved children, and live in love, as Christ loved us and gave himself up for us, a fragrant offering and sacrifice to God. (Ephesians 4:29-5:7)

When group members share conflicting ideas or opinions, you'll need a process by which to manage the situation. Here is a ten-step process that will help your group work through conflict in a productive and healthy way:

1. Remind the group of the overall goal.
Keeping the group's objectives in front of them is critical to reaching the best outcome. It's easy to get caught up in the "ideas" themselves and take our eyes off the ultimate goal. We want to get to the best possible solution that will help us achieve our shared objectives. This also serves to remind the members that they are a team, working toward a common goal.

2. Listen carefully to each person's idea.
Don't dismiss any idea. Sometimes the best outcome develops out of a small piece of one idea combined with a small piece of another. Always look for the value in each idea. Find a positive comment to make about each idea before moving on to the next. This will ensure that every person feels "heard" and respected.

3. Expect team members to support their positions with data and facts.
This doesn't necessarily mean numbers; just make sure group members can support their ideas with clear, logical reasoning. The purpose isn't to give them the burden of substantiating the validity of their points; it is to help other members of the group understand the background and benefits of their positions.

4. Ask questions to gain understanding.
Again, the purpose here is to make sure you and the rest of the team understand the person's position clearly. This also gives the individual an opportunity to clarify or flesh-out his or her thoughts.

5. *Clarify points of mutual agreement.*

This step is critical for reaching the optimal outcome. Identifying the points of mutual agreement will serve to remind the group of their shared purpose and is necessary for synergy to take place.

6. *Consider the benefits and pitfalls of each idea.*

It is helpful to do this in the group, listing the "pros and cons" of each idea on a board if possible. The goal here is not to rule out any idea but to identify the merits and disadvantages of each one in order to develop the *best* solution. This step sets the stage for the next part of the process.

7. *Take time to process, reflect, and think.*

Unless it is absolutely impossible, we recommend that you *not* attempt to reach resolution in one meeting. Set up a date and time to get back together to continue the discussion, and encourage all members to prayerfully reflect and think about all the ideas discussed. This allows emotions to cool down if they've become elevated, enabling everyone to think more clearly and practically at the next meeting. Often new (and better) ideas or solutions will arise once everyone has had an opportunity to process and "live with" the ideas that have already been presented. Each individual will typically begin to recognize some faults in his or her own position as well as the merits of someone else's.

8. *Encourage the group to consider new approaches that incorporate the best of all ideas.*

Ask for any new thoughts or ideas that occurred to anyone, and begin brainstorming possible new approaches. You're looking for synergy here, which means that the group process generates a solution that is better than any of the options put forth by any given individual.

9. *Discuss the various options and come to agreement about which approach to take.*

At this point you might want to identify a number of workable options and have people discuss each one. Remind the group that once a decision has been made, the group expects the full support of each member on the team. Now is the time for any dissent to be expressed—not in the hallways afterwards. Depending on how many ideas rise to the top as "potential options," the group may reach consensus through discussion, or you may need to take a vote.

10. *Recognize and reward those group members who shared their ideas.*

Do this sincerely and publicly. If you want people to continue to share their ideas and support the group process, working through conflict in healthy productive ways, you must show appreciation for those who do so. Trust me; they will appreciate it, even if their ideas aren't the ones adopted.

For a biblical example of this process, read the account of the Council at Jerusalem (Acts 15:1-30). There was much debate, with both sides supporting their positions with examples and Scripture passages. Consensus was reached whereby Gentiles were accepted into the body of believers without the requirement of first converting to Judaism. It is a powerful account of healthy, productive conflict management.

Preserving Unity of Spirit

Conflict can be positive. For some reason, our concept of conflict tends to be negative, and we think of it as something that should be avoided at all costs. In reality, though, healthy conflict can lead to deeper relationships and more productive ministry teams. Conflict has always existed and will always exist—even in the church. It's not whether we have conflict but how we approach it that sets us apart from the world. As we address conflict, we simply need to keep one thing in the front of our minds: In all things, love.

Finally, all of you, have unity of spirit, sympathy, love for one another, a tender heart, and a humble mind. (1 Peter 3:8)

What does that mean? How do we preserve unity of spirit in the midst of conflict? We do so by keeping in mind that, above all things, our faith in the risen Christ unites us in purpose. It is possible to love a person without agreeing with him or her. We can accept our differences and appreciate one another. Often our greatest achievements and closest friendships develop as we work together to do more than we could do alone, and this inevitably involves conflict. Handled with love and respect, conflict can be the most productive tool we possess.

Questions for Reflection or Discussion

1. How do misunderstandings or miscommunication contribute to interpersonal conflicts?

2. Discuss how working through interpersonal conflicts might lead to closer, deeper relationships.

3. Why is the *lack* of conflict not "good" for team ministries? Why do we struggle with that concept so much?

4. What can you do to create and contribute to an environment of open dialogue and idea-sharing on the teams in which you are involved?

CHAPTER 9

Leading Change and Encouraging Innovation

Do not remember the former things, or consider the things of old.
I am about to do a new thing; now it springs forth, do you not perceive it?
I will make a way in the wilderness and rivers in the desert. (Isaiah 43:19)

Change is invigorating…and scary. In September 1994, I (Yvonne) accepted a new job in Kansas City, which would move my family a thousand miles from our home in Georgia. While my husband and I were excited about the opportunities and benefits this new position would provide for our family, we were nervous as well. We would need to sell our home, he would have to find a new job, and we would need to get our children settled. Oh yeah—the children!

At the time, my daughter Dominique was a freshman in high school, and my son John was ten years old. When we sat down with them to tell them about the possibility of moving, the reaction was immediate and emotional—tears, anger, and outright refusal to even consider it. Not exactly the response we were hoping for!

We kept talking, and eventually they both came to accept that change was going to happen. We began to work through how the change would occur—when, where, and what role they would play. My daughter wanted to wait until after marching band season was over, and my son wanted to make sure he would be able to return to visit friends and family regularly. They both wanted to take part in selecting the house we would buy in our new location.

My husband agreed to stay in Georgia until spring so that Dominique could finish marching season, and we purchased three round trip plane tickets in advance for John. I loaded up the car and drove to Kansas City to live in temporary housing until they followed me after the first of the year. When they came to visit, we went house shopping together and we were unanimous in our choice of a home to move into permanently.

Everything didn't go perfectly, of course. There was the issue of making new friends, realizing that snowflakes didn't automatically mean school was cancelled in the Midwest, and missing family and friends in Georgia. Twelve years later, though, the children are grown, living on their own, and consider Kansas City home. If you asked either of them (and I have), they will tell you that the move was a very positive experience for them—opening their minds up to new possibilities as well as making them more independent, self-confident, and resilient.

Reflect on the changes that you've experienced in your own life—a move, a new job, a new skill acquired, a loss, or a reprioritization of values or activities. Describe here a change you experienced that was challenging at the time but rewarding or valuable in the end.

What happened? How did you respond? What did you learn from the experience? How has it shaped who you are today?

A God of Change

As humans, most of us dislike change—unless we're in control of the change, that is! Even if we're not happy with the current situation, we're nervous that change could make things worse.

In a sermon I heard recently, the pastor was preaching about resistance to change in the church, and he said something that struck me: Standing securely in our comfort zones, "we can make an idol out of stability." Wow. I had not considered that before, but it rings true. We're comfortable, and then something (or someone—God) comes along and moves us out of our comfort zones. We resist the change simply because it is change without considering that change may be a good thing.

God has been moving people out of their comfort zones since time began. Think about it for a minute: Do you believe Abram was "comfortable" with the change God asked him to agree to—packing up his family to go to some undefined "promised land"? Or what about when God told Noah to start building an ark when there was no rain in the forecast? Although we don't read of their discomfort in the Bible, it had to exist. They were human, after all. It is crystal clear that Moses wasn't comfortable when God called him to return to Egypt and lead his people out of captivity. And the early church was decidedly uncomfortable when Gentiles began to follow the Way and wanted to join the body of believers. The willingness of the early church to accept change enabled you and I to be part of this body called Christians.

There are numerous passages of scripture promising change or encouraging us to be open to change. Here are just a few:

I am about to create new heavens and a new earth; the former things shall not be remembered or come to mind. (Isaiah 65:17)

A new heart I will give you, and a new spirit I will put within you… (Ezekiel 36:26a)

[Jesus] said, "Truly I tell you, unless you change and become like children, you will never enter the kingdom of heaven.'" (Matthew 18:3)

Do not be conformed to this world, but be transformed by the renewing of your minds, so that you may discern what is the will of God - what is good and acceptable and perfect. (Romans 12:2)

So if anyone is in Christ, there is a new creation: everything old has passed away; see, everything has become new! (2 Corinthians 5:17)

Change is a hallmark of God's work in the world, and it is inevitable. There's an old saying: "The only constant is change." That means we must get comfortable with stepping outside our comfort zones. A pastor encouraged one congregation to make this their prayer: "Oh God, help me be comfortable with being uncomfortable!" As leaders, we have an important part to play. Our role is to facilitate change and help those we lead to navigate through their discomfort—even as we are navigating through our own. Alan Nelson writes: "Leadership would be unnecessary in an unchanging environment; management and administration would do" (*Leading Ideas*, Group Publishing, 2003, p. 26).

Let's consider why we're so averse to change and how a leader can make the process of change easier.

Barriers to Change

There are many factors working against change at any given point in time, but the most common ones include the following:

◆ lack of understanding about the need for change
◆ fear of the unknown
◆ insufficient resources to accomplish the change

Insufficient resources may or may not be within your control as a leader, but the first two—lack of understanding about the need for change and fear of the unknown—are things that you can address.

Occasionally, people are genuinely unaware that change is needed. From their perhaps incomplete perspective, things are working fine. They may not have enough information to give them the full picture for why change is desirable.

One ministry team leader I know was fast approaching burn-out. This was true not only of the leader, but also of all the team members. They were under tremendous pressure to provide a continuous amount of support for a ministry department, and, wanting to serve sacrificially, they gave 110 percent effort to everything they were asked to do. In fact, they gave until they began to drop with exhaustion. Finally the ministry leader had to approach the department head and communicate the problem clearly. The team wanted to serve, but it could not continue to provide the same level of service without either a break or additional resources. Things needed to change.

The ministry department head was caught off guard. The team members had done such a terrific job of serving that the physical and emotional toll their service was taking had been completely hidden from the department head. She didn't have a complete perspective. Working together, the group has begun to find solutions to the problem.

In other instances, people may recognize that change is needed but still be anxious about it. They wonder: How will the change affect me? What if I fail in the new environment? What if the change makes me unnecessary? They fear a loss of control, even if it's only perception and not reality.

> # In other instances, people may recognize that change is needed but still be anxious about it.

The department that I lead at work is a fast-paced, exciting one. The people who work for me tend to get promoted because although the pace is frenetic and the demands are high, they learn a great deal about the business. About a year ago, I asked one of my staff members to consider a transfer to another, smaller department.

She was nervous and concerned: was this request due to non-performance on her part or personality issues? I explained that this move was designed to help her new supervisor out of a tough spot and would serve her career goals quite well. Because the new department was smaller, she would be working even more closely with the department head and would be required to stretch herself. I shared with her that I believed she had great potential and that this move would give her an opportunity to grow quickly. She would have my support and the support of her new boss. We would work together to help her succeed.

She accepted the challenge and is happy she did so. She is developing professionally and personally in her new position. She just needed a little reassurance that the change would be for the better.

In most cases, a leader can successfully rally his or her team behind a needed change. All that is needed is a little planning and a lot of communicating.

A Process for Leading Change

Gaining the support of a team for an impending or hoped-for change seems challenging when you don't know where to begin. Following is a six-step process for leading a group through change. The steps are not sequential, and the time spent working through each step will vary in different situations. In fact, some of the steps will be ongoing throughout the entire transition. Each one, however, is essential.

1. Communicate the Need for Change

Kerry A. Bunker and Michael Wakefield, authors of *Leading with Authenticity in Times of Transition,* say that leaders need to communicate *relentlessly* (Greensboro, N.C.: Center for Creative Leadership Press, 2005). This critical first step will be ongoing throughout the change process. Keep in mind that communication is a two-way street. First, explain *what* the realities of the current situation are, *why* continuing with the status quo is not an acceptable alternative, and *how* the change will make things better. Help the group understand that although change is uncomfortable, it is necessary. Poet Kathleen Norris has said that "disconnecting from change does not recapture the past. It loses the future" (*Dakota: A Spiritual Geography,* Ticknor and Fields, 1993, chp. 9).

The next step is to listen. Allow people an opportunity to ask questions and express their concerns, doubts, and fears. Be willing to share your own discomfort while remaining steadfast in your commitment to the change. If you express confidence in the team's ability to handle change successfully even as you acknowledge that change is uncertain and sometimes risky, your authenticity will quell any worries that you're blind to the challenges the group will face. Concerns are easier to keep in proper perspective once they're expressed and acknowledged. At regular intervals, even after the team has accepted the need for change, remind them of why they're doing this and of the positive impact the change will bring.

2. Enlist Advocates for Change

It is helpful to have a group of key supporters who will serve as advocates and ambassadors for change. When confronted with resistance or criticism, they will respond with a positive message about the change, acting as a counterpoint to the naysayers while offering encouragement to those who may be fence-sitting. Enlist their help. Keep these key supporters well informed so that they will be prepared to respond to questions or concerns.

3. Share a Vision for the Future

Encouraging change isn't enough to get everyone on board; you must paint a picture of the future. People are more willing to adopt change if they understand how things will be better afterward. Give the group a mental image of the future that appeals to their sense of "what could be." Leadership consultants and authors James Kouzes and Barry Posner write: "Without vision, little could happen. All enterprises or projects, big or small, begin in the mind's eye; they begin with imagination and with the belief that what's merely an image can one day be real" (*The Leadership Challenge*, Josey-Bass Publishers, 1995, p. 93).

4. Authorize Others to Plan and Implement the Change

I've learned from experience that the best way to gain "buy-in" from a group is to include them in the process of planning and implementing the change. Once you've shared the vision for the future, empower your team to work together to figure out the best way to get there. This is crucial to bringing about change in any group.

Remember the fears mentioned earlier—the fear of loss of control and the fear of being unnecessary? Including people in the process from the beginning and giving them some real authority to make decisions will give them time to adapt to the prospect of change and combat some of those fears. John Kotter, Harvard Business School professor, writes: "Major internal transformation rarely happens unless many people assist. Yet employees generally won't help, or can't help, if they feel relatively powerless. Hence the relevance of empowerment." (*Leading Change* [Boston: Harvard Business School Press, 1996], p. 102).

5. Establish Milestones

Any big change seems more achievable if you establish short-term goals. Several years ago I, determined to finally lose the extra weight I'd been carrying for many years, went on a diet. Losing almost one hundred pounds seemed an insurmountable obstacle; but losing ten pounds seemed more attainable. And that's exactly how I did it—ten pounds at a time. At each milestone, I treated myself in some way: a new outfit, a new haircut, and so forth.

The same principle holds true with leading a group through change. Help them see the progress they're making—it's absolutely necessary in order to maintain momentum, especially in a long-term change process.

My company has been going through change over the past eighteen months. Every once in a while someone will say, "Nothing's changed. We're not getting anywhere!" We have to pause to reflect and remember how far we've come. We may not have reached the finish line yet, but we are a long way from where we started.

6. Celebrate Successes

Make a special occasion out of achieving your short-term goals. Celebrate when people step out of their comfort zones. Recognize effort and positive attitude. What you're looking for here is public attention to forward momentum. It provides energy and fuels excitement. Celebrations afford you the opportunity to say, "Well done," which makes it more likely that you'll get support for your next initiative. Most people are more motivated by recognition and appreciation than by money or other tangible rewards. When you're leading a group in the church and they're volunteering, that may be all you have to offer anyway!

Encouraging Innovation

Let's talk a moment about another barrier to change—*you*. Have you heard the saying that originated in an old "Pogo" cartoon by Walt Kelly: "We have met the enemy, and he is us"? Sometimes the leader of a group unintentionally creates barriers to change and innovation. This may be because he or she helped to create the current processes and thus feels emotionally committed to the status quo, or it may be because he or she tends to create an environment that stifles creativity.

> **People will not bring new ideas to you, especially ones that require leaving behind the status quo, if they believe you will react negatively.**

I've certainly experienced the former situation. For a number of years, I led the spiritual gifts team at our church. Carol and I coauthored the curriculum *Serving from the Heart*, which is designed to be taught in four- or eight-week formats. When team members suggested that we might reach additional people by offering two-week sessions, I was slightly offended. *What did they mean by saying that some people might not be willing to commit to four or eight weeks?* I wondered. It took a long time for me to get past my personal feelings and look at the situation objectively. Now the team offers spiritual gifts discovery classes in a variety of formats and reaches many more people in the process.

As leaders, we need to create an environment conducive to thinking outside the box—one that welcomes new ideas. We need not only to allow but also to encourage others to challenge our thinking and existing processes. Sometimes we just need new people and the fresh eyes they bring to the team to shake things up a little bit. We need to stay in touch with the "customer." Regularly ask yourself this question: Is what we're doing meeting the needs of our audience? What you are doing may have met their needs three years ago, but does it still do so?

So, how do you create an environment that encourages innovation? First, you must develop trust. Trust is imperative. People will not bring new ideas to you, especially ones that require leaving behind the status quo, if they believe you will react negatively. I tend to be pretty opinionated, so I've adopted a technique that helps me to think more objectively: I delay my response. When someone comes to me with an idea to which my first reaction is negative, I always ask for time to think it over. I will say honestly that I have some reservations and that I need a day or two to consider the idea and its implications carefully.

This technique accomplishes several things. First, it prevents me from responding emotionally. It gets me out of the moment and gives me time to be more objective. Second, it demonstrates to those I lead that I will give their ideas respectful consideration. Third, even if I eventually respond by suggesting a modification to their idea or by declining to implement their idea, I am able to articulate my reasoning clearly without squelching their creativity.

Another process I recommend you adopt is to regularly ask the group this question: What could we improve by doing things differently? Again, I have found that if I am the one who raises this question, it creates a more open atmosphere—both on the part of the team members, who perceive me as being open to new ideas, and on my own part, because I am naturally more receptive to ideas I have invited others to share.

Review all of your current processes and consider whether they still serve your audience as effectively as they did in the past. Think about how your audience may have changed over time. Are their needs the same, or have those needs changed, too? What new resources and technology are available now that you didn't have before? How might utilizing them make your ministry more efficient or effective?

Avoid at all costs these creativity-squelching comments:
We've tried that before, and it didn't work.
> Remember, things may have changed since the last time you tried it.
> What did you learn last time that might enable it to succeed this time?

We do it this way around here, and it works for us.
> Are you guilty of the "not invented here" syndrome? In other words, if it's not your idea, it's not a good idea. Listen, ask questions, and find out if a new way of doing things might be better.

It's just not practical or *We can't afford it.*
> Instead, ask the group what can be done to make it practical or affordable. What might need to change to make it work? Perhaps it won't work in the current situation, but with a little tweak here and a little tweak there, you may have a workable idea.

It's a good idea, but...
> Stop with "It's a good idea." Then state the issues or obstacles the group needs to address. Ask the group how those things could be overcome. Let them think about it and own their ideas.

You get the idea. Don't kill creativity; ignite it. Make a habit of questioning the status quo. That doesn't mean you should embrace change for the sake of change. What you're looking for is change that makes things better—more effective, more manageable, more efficient, and so forth. As your team members see that you are open to change and new ideas and experience your leadership through transitions, they will become more comfortable with being uncomfortable. In other words, they will become more open to change and new ideas themselves. Your goal as leader is to create an environment that allows creativity to flow so that your team may see possibilities. In *The Art of Possibility*, Rosamunde and Benjamin Zander tell this story that illustrates how "possibility thinking" makes a world of difference in how you perceive reality (Penguin Books, 2000, p. 9):

A shoe factory sends two marketing scouts to a region of Africa to study the prospects for expanding business. One sends back a telegram saying,
SITUATION HOPELESS. STOP. NO ONE WEARS SHOES.

The other writes back triumphantly,
GLORIOUS BUSINESS OPPORTUNITY. STOP. THEY HAVE NO SHOES.

How can you encourage your team to see past what is, to what might be?

Questions for Reflection or Discussion

1. What is your church's current process for change? How are new ideas introduced, approved, and implemented?

2. Discuss a change that was poorly received and/or implemented. What went wrong? What could have been done differently to achieve a better outcome?

3. Describe a past transition that you view as a success. What obstacles to change had to be overcome? How was that accomplished? What did the leader(s) of the change do to enlist the support of team members?

4. What can you do in the next thirty days to foster an innovative environment (one that sees "possibilities") in the team(s) you lead?

Developing the Next Generation of Leaders

The next day Moses sat as judge for the people, while the people stood around him from morning until evening. When Moses' father-in-law saw all that he was doing for the people, he said, "What is this that you are doing for the people? Why do you sit alone, while all the people stand around you from morning until evening? ...What you are doing is not good. You will surely wear yourself out, both you and these people with you. For the task is too heavy for you; you cannot do it alone." (Exodus 18:13-14, 17b-18)

Without even realizing it, many of us share Moses' natural tendency in leadership—we try to do it all ourselves. Sometimes we believe the responsibility is ours alone. Maybe we like being in charge. We enjoy feeling needed. Many times we simply don't know how to lead differently. If we haven't been taught shared leadership by experience or example, it is difficult to put this concept into practice.

Moses was in just that situation. God had put him in charge, and he was fulfilling his obligation to lead as he understood it. He knew the people were frustrated with waiting in line for him, but he didn't quite know what else to do. Thank goodness his father-in-law, Jethro, came to visit! He taught Moses a model for shared leadership, encouraging Moses to find some God-fearing, trustworthy people, train them, and appoint them to serve as judges for segments of the people. Then Moses could handle the difficult cases and spend the rest of his time doing more productive things. Jethro told Moses how this would benefit both Moses and the people: "If you do this, and God so commands you, then you will be able to endure, and all these people will go to their home in peace" (Exodus 18:23). In other words, the judges would share the responsibility of leadership with Moses, enabling him to avoid burnout, and the people would receive the attention they needed faster. Everyone would be happier!

Consider the various leaders you have known. Did any of them follow Moses' "I'm supposed to do it all" leadership model? What type of environment did that create? How did it make you feel?

Perhaps you have had some wise leaders like Jethro, who shared their leadership. What type of environment did that create? How did it affect you?

Shared Leadership Is Biblical Leadership

The Bible is rife with examples of shared leadership. This doesn't mean that no one is really "in charge," it simply means that leadership isn't meant to be a burden carried alone. In fact, a leader has an obligation to encourage and equip others to lead with him or her.

In many cases Scripture goes beyond the general concept of shared leadership to the intentional process of choosing and developing an apprentice. Our definition of *apprentice* is someone who works alongside an experienced leader to learn the expectations of the role and to develop the skills necessary to fulfill it. Moses prepared Joshua to take over for him after his death. Elijah mentored Elisha until he was ready to assume a leadership role. Barnabas did the same for John Mark, and Paul mentored and coached Timothy.

> **A leader has an obligation to encourage and equip others to lead with him or her.**

Why is this important? If you've ever experienced a situation in which a leader suddenly left and no one was prepared to take over the leadership role, you understand exactly what happens: chaos (at least temporarily). There might be a complete leadership vacuum, in which no one is in place who can fill the role; or perhaps there is someone in place, but he or she is not thoroughly equipped, leaving that individual feeling overwhelmed and ill-prepared to lead. Either way, it is not a good situation.

Imagine instead a situation where the leader has been sharing leadership with an apprentice for a year. This person has had practice fulfilling some of the responsibilities of the role, and has received feedback and coaching to improve his or her performance. Now when the leader suddenly leaves, the apprentice is not only qualified to step up, but he or she is also mentally and emotionally prepared to do so. The transition is much more likely to go smoothly, which is better for the organization, those being led, and those being served.

Okay, so we're in agreement that sharing leadership and developing an apprentice are good ideas. Now, how do you do it? There are five steps (though steps 3-5 are connected and frequently overlap):

◆ Identify potential leaders.
◆ Invite one or more to share leadership with you as an apprentice.
◆ Equip your apprentice(s) to lead.
◆ Coach the new leader(s) to reach maximum effectiveness.
◆ Release your apprentice(s) to lead independently.

Identifying Potential Leaders

As you begin to look for people with leadership potential, how do you identify a good candidate? First and foremost, a candidate should have the appropriate spiritual gift(s). The gifts required will depend somewhat on the role or position the potential leader will fill, but he or she definitely should possess a leadership gift. This doesn't mean only the spiritual gift of "leadership"; it includes any gift that qualifies a person for a leadership role, such as administration, teaching, pastor-teacher, and so forth. Once you've determined that a person has the requisite gifts for leadership, be on the lookout for these other qualities:

Willingness to Assume Responsibility and Follow Through – Look for people who step up to the plate and take on responsibility when needed. These people not only take charge but also follow a project through to completion. Sometimes these people just see themselves as "worker-bees," but one cannot be a leader without the willingness to take on a project and see that it gets done.

A Healthy Dose of Constructive Criticism – Leaders (and potential leaders) are often dissatisfied with the status quo. They always think things could be done better. That doesn't mean you should look for people who are constantly complaining (in fact, these people are often not suited for leadership). Instead, look for those who offer constructive ideas for improvement in the organization or ministry.

Practicality – You want to find people who offer practical feedback and ideas. A person who has lots of ideas, none of which are even remotely workable, probably isn't the ideal candidate for potential leadership.

Vision – A leader needs to have a vision or picture for the future of the organization and be able to communicate that vision effectively to others so that they can pursue it together.

People Magnets – Leaders, even before they are in official leadership positions, often have the ability to influence others. People gravitate toward natural leaders. Others want to spend time with them. Their advice is sought on important issues. When they speak or offer ideas, other people listen to and respect them.

Confidence and Determination – Look for people who have conviction and perhaps even are a little "thick-skinned." Leaders face obstacles every day. They must have the determination necessary to overcome or work through those obstacles to accomplish their goals.

Potential leaders need both good character and leadership skills. In *Leading Life Changing Small Groups* (Zondervan Publishing, 1996, p. 70), Bill Donahue compares some of the differences in this way:

GOOD CHARACTER	LEADERSHIP SKILLS
Internal Measure	External Measure
Must be developed	Can be taught
About relationships to God & other people	About relationships to tasks
Takes time to develop	Takes time and practice to perfect
Lack of good character can disqualify from leadership	Lack of leadership skills can delay from leadership

As you identify people with leadership potential, remember that skills can be taught. People with little or no leadership experience may not possess all the skills they'll need to be successful. With your guidance and a little practice, they can develop those skills. We recommend, however, that you do not invite people who exhibit poor character to serve in leadership roles. They will set a poor example for others.

When you have identified the persons you believe have leadership potential, it's time to actually invite them to begin the journey into leadership as an apprentice. Start this process with prayer. Before you make the invitation, pray for yourself and the person you're inviting. Pray that the Holy Spirit will guide your thoughts and conversation, and that the person being invited will listen for and hear God's call into leadership, if there is one. Sometimes people don't hear that calling; other times it simply isn't the right time in their lives to assume a leadership role. You have to be open to your invitation being declined. That's okay.

The next step is to meet with the individual for an initial discussion. Spell out the qualities and gifts you see that convince you of his or her leadership potential. Clarify your expectations in writing with a position description, using the worksheet provided in the Appendix (p. 138). Make sure that the person understands what is required, and that he or she is committed to the process. Don't soft-sell the position. Explain the process you will use to prepare him or her for leadership, including the method and time frame for equipping, when you'll meet again to evaluate how it's going and whether to continue, and what he or she can expect from you as a coach.

Finally, ask the person to pray about your invitation. Don't expect someone to make a commitment like this on the spur of the moment. Give him or her time to consider the implications for family and leisure time. This is a serious (though not reversible) decision and should be taken as such. If the individual has a family, he or she will want to include them in the decision process. You want them included too, because family support is critical for a leader.

Equipping for Leadership

In preparing someone to lead, take advantage of how adults learn most effectively. We remember 10 percent of what we hear, 50 percent of what we see, 70 percent of what we say, and 90 percent of what we do. That translates into an interactive equipping process, where the person being equipped has lots of opportunities to practice what he or she is being taught. In the beginning, he or she will make a few mistakes. You must offer grace and exhibit patience, providing a safe environment for your apprentice to fail, learn from those failures, and get back up and try again.

We use a five-stage process for equipping someone for leadership. Remember that equipping someone is a fluid experience. By that we mean that while you generally progress from one stage to the next, the stages often overlap. Sometimes you'll be in one stage of the process of equipping for one skill while you're in a different stage of the process for another. Notice that sharing the vision and values of the organization is part of every step prior to releasing for leadership. This is because you want the apprentice to learn to make his or her own decisions using the vision and values of the organization as a guiding light and boundary markers. If he or she doesn't know and understand what the organization stands for, this won't be possible.

Model: *I do, you watch.*

> In stage one, model the *behaviors* and *attitudes* you want your apprentice to learn. Give him or her an example to follow. Have the apprentice shadow you to see what is involved in the role you will be training him or her to fill. Share the vision and values of the organization. Help the apprentice grasp what the organization stands for and believes in, as well as its purpose for existence. Clearly communicate how the role contributes to that purpose so he or she can see how the two are connected.

Mentor: *I do, you watch, we talk.*

> In stage two, continue to share the vision and values of the organization. During this stage, you will continue to model the behaviors and attitudes you want the apprentice to learn, explaining not only the "what" but also the "why" of everything you do. Encourage the

apprentice to ask questions, and in turn, you ask questions, too, about how he or she will do these tasks, what support or training he or she might need, and so forth.

Partner: *We do together.*
> In stage three, give your apprentice small responsibilities to share with you. Serve as a backup and resource for him or her in case you're needed. During this stage you want your apprentice to begin getting more comfortable (or at least less nervous!) in a leadership role. This also gives you an opportunity to provide feedback and encouragement and to correct any missteps or inappropriate behaviors and attitudes you see in a loving manner. Continue to share the vision and values of the organization.

Coach: *You do, I guide.*
> In stage four, you'll give increasingly larger responsibilities to your apprentice. Provide feedback and encouragement. When he or she comes to you with questions, don't give the answers outright; instead, ask questions to guide the individual to clarity or to resources where he or she can find the answers independently. Remember, your role is to prepare your apprentice to fly solo. Continue to share the vision and values of the organization. This stage overlaps with stage five and continues throughout the individual's service. We'll talk a little more in depth about coaching at the end of this section.

Release: *You do, I applaud.*
> In stage five, the individual is ready to lead independently. He or she will still come to you with questions, and you will serve as an important resource and sounding board. Continue to provide feedback and encouragement to help the new leader improve his or her leadership skills. Give the leader three things every leader deserves: responsibility, authority, and accountability.

Ongoing Coaching for Development

Coaching for development usually revolves around a set of specific skills, which vary depending on the position of the person being coached. It involves teaching, training, and supervising, and it is more about asking the right questions than imparting information. There are three important parts: pre-event coaching, event observation, and post-event coaching. In this context, event refers to any project, situation, meeting, or communication. Outlines for you to use for each of these three coaching opportunities are provided in the Appendix (pp. 139-141).

Pre-event coaching: In the beginning of your coaching relationship, you'll spend a lot of time in this area. Ask questions such as these:

- What do you plan to do?
- How will you get it done?
- Why do you choose to do it that way?
- Who will you involve?
- What will you ask them to contribute?
- What do you expect to happen?
- How can I help?

As the individual responds, you may need to ask follow-up questions to probe deeper or re-direct him or her, such as "Have you considered...?" Or "What will you do if _____ happens?" The goal here is to make sure that you understand the plan, that it is in alignment with the vision and values of the organization, and that the apprentice has the resources he or she needs to complete the task well.

Event Observation: During the event, your role is to notice what happens—both what is done well and what could be improved. If your apprentice is experiencing difficulty, find out if he or she needs assistance but do not take over.

Post-event coaching: After the event, set up a time to get together. It's important to schedule this meeting one-on-one, and as close to the event date as possible, so it's still fresh in both your minds. Begin with asking the apprentice what he or she thinks went well, and then add to his or her observations anything in addition that you feel should be celebrated. This includes efforts or outcomes that demonstrate growth, even if not completely successful. Follow this by asking the individual what could be improved upon and how he or she proposes doing so, as well as what you can do to help. Usually the individual will know what went wrong, and it's easier if he or she names it instead of you pointing it out. However, if the apprentice didn't notice a problem that you did, explain what you observed and give your suggestions for doing better next time.

Five Common Mistakes Leaders Make When Developing Other Leaders

In his book *The Top Ten Mistakes Leaders Make* (Victor Books, 2004), Hans Finzel describes common leadership pitfalls. Although all of the mistakes he discusses have validity, five are critical to avoid when developing future leaders. Remember, your apprentice will be learning from your example. The mistakes you make in leading are likely to be perpetuated in the apprentice's leadership, too.

1. Prioritizing Projects Over People

Sometimes we get so caught up in getting things done that we forget we are leading people. While the projects do need to get done, our first priority as leaders should be taking care of the people we lead. This means noticing when something isn't right with their moods or physical health. It means stopping in the midst of activity to pray with them, encourage them, or perhaps even celebrate a great success in their lives. People first, projects second—always!

2. Absence of Affirmation

Sometimes we get so busy that we forget to praise someone for a job well done. Remember, no news is not good news when you're leading people. They want to hear that they are doing okay, that you're pleased with the work they're doing, and that you appreciate their time and efforts.

3. Top-down Management and Decisions

In the short term, it may actually seem to be easier just to do everything yourself. Don't fall into that trap. In the long run, sharing leadership with someone who is well prepared to lead will benefit you and the organization in more ways than you can even imagine. You will regain some of that time lost in the equipping process as you are free to do other things. You also will gain a trusted resource and partner.

Sharing leadership means including others in setting the direction and making important decisions. A dictatorship, even a benevolent one, is not a good management approach if you want to prepare others to lead. It may take longer to reach a decision in a group process, but usually the decisions are of much better quality and include ideas that one person never would have thought of alone. Of course, if you are working with someone who has assumed a significant amount of responsibility for a part of the organization, he or she should be the ultimate decision-maker for that group. He or she will have to carry out the decisions made and thus should have rights to determine how the work gets done. That doesn't mean that the person should make decisions in a vacuum; it simply means that the individual should be allowed to make the final call.

4. Dirty Delegation

This term refers to delegating only the jobs you don't want to do… the unglamorous "grunt" work. A good leader gives the people he or she leads opportunities to serve on high visibility projects, raising their self-esteem and giving them exposure to other leaders in the organization.

5. Chaos in Communication

Make sure you are communicating effectively. Ask questions to ensure you're understood. Follow up on verbal conversations with a short e-mail to confirm decisions made or actions to be taken, along with timelines. It is also critical that you communicate the big picture—what's happening in the organization outside of your group—so that your group feels connected to the entire organization. Keeping your group informed will make them feel part of the whole.

Five Leadership "Musts"

1. Be Available

How much time is required? That depends on what sort of role you are preparing your apprentice to assume. All of your communication doesn't need to be face to face. You just need to make yourself available, and then give the person 100 percent of your attention when needed.

Meet with the individual you're equipping on a regular basis outside of official "work" time. Get together for coffee or a cola once a month just to "chat." Many times an important question or issue will surface during in an informal setting more easily than it will in an official one. If the person calls on the phone or sends an e-mail, take the time to converse or respond promptly. Let the person know he or she can count on you to be there when you are needed.

2. Build Trust

Every apprentice deserves your authenticity. You must build a relationship of open communication and trust. This happens only over time, and only if you set the example. As the leader, you must be the first to be authentic and vulnerable, modeling the behavior and attitudes you want from the apprentice. Show transparency in your strengths and weaknesses, and exhibit consistency in character.

3. Believe in People

Give encouragement until others believe in themselves. Dale Carnegie said that a leader should give people "a fine reputation to live up to" (*How to Win Friends and Influence People*, (Simon & Schuster, 1981, p. 259). In their book *The Art of Possibility*, Rosamund and Benjamin Zander call this "giving everyone an A." According to the Zanders, "This A is not an expectation to live up to, but a possibility to live into" (Penguin Books, 2000, p. 26). This means giving an encouraging word even when someone doesn't perform up to your expectations, as well as when he or she performs perfectly but things still don't go as planned. Your job is to keep hope and enthusiasm high.

4. Add Significance

Give people important, meaningful work to do. Help them see how what they do is serving a greater purpose. Leaders don't want to just be "busy," they want to contribute to something that matters!

5. Provide Security

Establish a support system of resources and fellow leaders for the individual to call on when needed. Make sure your apprentice doesn't feel you've thrown him or her in the deep end of the pool with a "sink or swim" attitude. Give the individual confidence by supporting him or her with your presence at projects or events he or she is managing.

What If He or She Doesn't Work Out?

Occasionally, despite the best efforts of your apprentice and yourself, things just don't work out. You find yourself in the position of having to tell someone that leadership in a particular role is not a good fit for him or her. There is no easy way through this—it will be difficult and uncomfortable.

When you believe an apprentice is not qualified for leadership, your first step should be to pray. Then discuss the situation with someone who serves as a coach or mentor to you. Make certain your judgment is sound and not predicated on a personality conflict. Review the expectations for leadership laid out in the position description you used during the invitation to apprenticeship. Which ones are not being met? Why? Sometimes a person may have the right gifts and skills, but because of other things happening in their lives, the timing is not right for leadership. Decide how to best communicate what you believe, and set up a time to meet face-to-face. Then pray some more!

At the meeting, begin by asking the individual how he or she feels things are going. You might say, "I've noticed you've been struggling with _____. Is everything okay?" I (Yvonne) have been in this situation a number of times and have been relieved to find that, when given an opening to bow out gracefully, the other person often has done the "uninviting" for me. Sometimes this won't happen, though, and you'll need to be prepared to clearly but lovingly communicate which expectations the person is not fulfilling. This will be much easier if you put those expectations in writing and share them during the invitation to apprenticeship. Allow the person a way to save face by offering an appropriate position in your group if possible. Remember that although this person is not right for a particular position of leadership at this time, he or she still deserves your respect and grace.

As a tool for making the invitation to apprenticeship, we've included a blank ministry position description in the Appendix (p. 138). Let's go over each of the sections, and then you may spend some time completing this tool for the apprentice position in which you will be inviting someone to serve.

◆ Responsibilities: What are the duties and responsibilities fulfilled by someone in this position? Be as thorough as possible!

◆ Spiritual Gifts: Which spiritual gifts are required or helpful for someone in this position?

◆ Talents/Skills: Which talents or skills will be necessary to fulfill this position? The person may possess some of these now; for some you may need to providing training or practice.

- ◆ Resources: This section refers to the amount of time required of someone in this role. "Length of commitment" refers to total time you're asking the individual to serve (one year, two years, and so forth). "Regular commitments" refers to any regular meetings or events the person will be required to attend. "Availability" refers to how much time per week the person can expect to spend in this role.
- ◆ Individuality: What personality traits or types might be best suited for this position?
- ◆ Dreams for: What should this person be passionate about? Where might he or she dream about making a difference?
- ◆ Experiences: What experiences might make this person uniquely qualified for this role?
- ◆ Minimum Spiritual Maturity: Consider the role the person will be filling. Will he or she be leading projects or people? Anyone leading in the church needs to have a life that demonstrates an active relationship with Christ and ongoing spiritual growth. This is especially true for someone leading people.
- ◆ Additional Comments: What formal training will be provided? What resources are available? Add any helpful information in this section.

Questions for Reflection or Discussion

1. In what ways have you been prepared for leadership? What steps or method did another leader or mentor use? Which of those were most effective?

2. If you weren't formally "trained" for leadership, what lessons did you learn through observing your own leaders? Which of those would you like to model for others?

3. Discuss which of the "leadership mistakes" you have observed in a leader in the past. What effect did that have?

4. Discuss which of the "leadership musts" you have observed in a leader in the past. How did that make you feel?

5. Discuss the impact coaching for performance improvement might have on an individual's leadership.

Keeping It All in Perspective

I myself will be the shepherd of my sheep, and I will make them lie down, says the Lord God. I will seek the lost, and will bring back the strayed, and I will bind up the injured, and I will strengthen the weak. (Ezekiel 34:15-16a)

In this passage from Ezekiel, we see God's definition of a good shepherd. That is exactly what we are called to be as leaders—shepherds over God's flock. We lead the way, seeking the lost, bringing them back into the fold, strengthening them, and helping them find wholeness and fulfillment.

Our focus for most of this book has been on the practical skills that you will need to lead effectively. As we close, we want to take you back to the beginning for a moment and remind you of the true purpose of a leader: to provide guidance and direction to a group of people. We are called to care for and feed—to influence and nurture—a portion of God's flock—God's people.

We have to maintain our focus on the people we lead, even as we work to accomplish the tasks before us. It is critical we never forget that our primary responsibility is the people. For some of them, you may be the only "official" leader they are connected to at church. They will judge how much the church cares about them by how much they perceive you care for them. You're probably familiar with the saying, "People don't care how much you know until they know how much you care."

That is especially true for leaders in the church. God, too, is watching to see how you care for your team. Recall the passage of scripture from 1 Samuel that opened the first chapter of this book:

> But the Lord said to Samuel, "Do not look on his appearance or on the height of his stature, because I have rejected him; for the Lord does not see as mortals see; they look on the outward appearance, but the Lord looks on the heart." (1 Samuel 16:7)

This passage relates the story of God's selection of David to lead Israel. A description of David's leadership is found in Psalm 78:72:

> With upright heart he tended them,
> And guided them with skillful hand.

Notice that, in God's eyes, an "upright heart" comes before a "skillful hand." Both God and the people you lead will evaluate your leadership first on the level of love you have for them, and then on your skill in leading. It is important to continually improve our leadership abilities, but we must keep our perspective in focus: With God, people come first.

This realization also has implications for you personally. God knows where your heart is, and God is merciful. If you don't do everything perfectly as a leader (and you won't, so go ahead and accept that), let it go. Don't berate yourself. Determine to do better next time, and then plan and prepare to do so.

Our hope is that this book will help you do just that. We pray God's richest blessings on your life and your leadership.

The Lord bless you and keep you;
the Lord make his face to shine upon you, and be gracious to you;
the Lord lift up his countenance upon you, and give you peace.
(Numbers 6:24-26)

APPENDIX

Ministry Planning Worksheet

Use the following template to evaluate how you plan to achieve a desired outcome that will help to bring about transformation in the lives of participants (discipleship).

Name of ministry:	
Ministry/class objective: *(This is the desired outcome for your participants and your church as a result of offering the ministry/class — perhaps your vision or mission statement for the ministry/class)*	
What can your participants expect from you and/or the ministry/class as a result of their involvement?	
What do you expect from your participants?	
How are the above expectations being communicated?	
How do you currently evaluate results?	
What results are you achieving?	
What will you do to enhance the ministry/class to achieve better results?	

AGENDA

*Purpose of Meeting:*_____

_____

_____

Opening:

    Connect:_____

    Prayer:_____

    Review of last meeting/action items:_____

Content:

What	Desired Outcome	Who	How	Time

Closing:

    Summary

    Review Action Steps / Who / Time

    Next Agenda

    Thanks / Celebration / Recognition

    Joys & Concerns and Prayer

Group Openers or Icebreakers

Group openers and icebreakers are designed to help group members get to know one another better and begin to build relationships. They should be open-ended questions, requiring more than simple yes and no answers.

Use good judgment when selecting an icebreaker. If your group is new, it's better to keep the questions "light" at this stage. As relationships develop in the group, begin to encourage people to open up more with in-depth questions that involve deeper thoughts and emotions.

Newer Groups

My favorite way to relax is…

What did you enjoy most about childhood?

If I could invent one gadget to make my life easier, I'd invent something that would…because…

What is your fondest memory of a holiday and why?

If your house was on fire, what three items (not people) would you try to save?

What was your first job? What do you remember most about it?

Who was the best or worst boss you ever had and why do you think so?

What was your first pet?

Describe a teacher who had a lasting influence on you.

Established Groups

Who do you go to for guidance in life and why?

If you had three wishes, what would you wish for?

What has been one of the greatest adventures you have ever been on?

What is one of the most memorable dreams you have ever had?

If you were going to leave the world one piece of advice before you died, what would it be?

What is the nicest thing anybody has ever said about you?

Which of your senses do you value most? Why?

If you were given a year sabbatical from work, what would you do?

If you had all the money, training, and talent needed, what would you choose to do for a living?

Well Established Groups

What one thing would you like your obituary to say about you? Why?

Where do you go or what do you do when you need to "recharge your batteries"? Why?

In what area of your life would you like to have greater peace? Why?

What is one of your biggest fears about the future?

Ministry Team Mission Statement Worksheet

Why is a mission statement important to every ministry team?
A team works best when everyone understands its purpose and goals. Reaching a common understanding of the mission will give your team a firm foundation. The mission statement should be clear, concise, and compelling.

A mission statement can help your team:
◆ Understand what the team is supposed to do and why—and what it should not do.
◆ Appreciate the importance of your team's role within the church.
◆ Evaluate challenges and celebrate successes.
◆ Communicate the work of your team to others outside the team.
◆ Focus its creativity, efforts, energy, and thinking.

Now it's time to get started. Answer these four questions on behalf of your team...

What do we call ourselves (what is the name of our team or ministry)?

_____

Who is our customer (who is being served by our ministry)?

_____

What do we do (how would we describe our ministry work)?

_____

Why do we do it (what is our motivation)?

_____

Our ministry team's mission statement...

Your final step: Be certain that the ministry team mission statement you create aligns with the mission statement of your church. Write the mission statement of your church here:

About Team Covenants

Purpose

Team covenants are designed for the purpose of holding members of a team mutually accountable to the group's mission, values, and expectations. Agreeing up front to the elements contained within the covenant will help the team stay on track, achieve its goals, and avoid potential conflict and/or frustration. In other words, a well-crafted covenant lays the foundation for a healthy team.

Content

Mission

First and foremost, teams should have a stated purpose for forming and meeting. The purpose of the team can be found in the mission statement of the team. (If the team has yet to craft a mission statement, use the resource found in this book to do so. See p. 120.) The mission statement is a tool to keep the team focused on its goals and objectives.

Values

Adhering to values will help to create a safe environment where team members feel appreciated and are free to express their challenges, triumphs, and ideas. Examples of values you may want to consider including in your covenant are:

◆ Confidentiality—when personal information is shared at team meetings
◆ Acceptance—of ideas, values, other persons
◆ Mutual respect—for fellow team members' thoughts and actions
◆ Honesty—team members must be able to trust one another
◆ Sensitivity—to the cares and needs of others
◆ Affirmation—of other member's gifts, abilities, and accomplishments
◆ Accountability—to attend meetings, be on time, accomplish assigned tasks
◆ Growth—creating an environment for spiritual and intellectual growth
◆ Others: _____

Expectations

Here is where you will list the ground rules for your team and team meetings. Logistical items might include:

◆ When, where, and how often you meet
◆ Attendance expectations
◆ Refreshments—if and when you have them and who provides
◆ Ways in which you might share team leadership (facilitating meetings, sending out agendas and reminders, providing a devotion, bringing refreshments, following up with absentees, leading prayer time, etc.)

The team leader should be prepared to facilitate the creation of the covenant. Despite all the guidelines previously given, you will want to keep your covenant simple. Once the team agrees on the written covenant, have every member sign and keep a personal copy. You may want to review the agreement at the end of six months to evaluate its effectiveness. You also will need to revisit the covenant when new people join the team.

Team Covenant Worksheet

1. The mission of our team is....

2. As individual members of the team, we agree to uphold the
   following values…

3. We will meet _____ from _____ to _____.
   (Use a format that makes sense for your group—if there are established
   meeting times, list those here.)

4. Regular attendance is important. If, however, a team member is unable to
   attend a meeting, the team leader will be called in advance. Team members
   will take responsibility for catching up on missed communication and work.

5. We agree to share leadership responsibilities by…

Signatures: _____   _____

            _____   _____

            _____   _____

            _____   _____

Date: _____

(Have all team members sign one copy. Make a copy of the signed document
   for each member.)

Vision Statement Writing Tool

Sample	Your draft
Ministry name: Small Groups	Ministry name:
List of preferred outcomes: ◆ Christ-centered ◆ Authentic community ◆ Spiritual growth ◆ Care for one another ◆ Sharing the love of Christ ◆ Serving the needs of others ◆ Making a difference in the world	List of preferred outcomes: ◆ Our ministry is _____ ◆ And _____ ◆ And _____ ◆ And _____ ◆ And _____ ◆ And _____ ◆ And _____
Do all the statements on this list align with the vision of the church? _X_ yes ___ no (if not, you will need to rework your vision statement until alignment is achieved)	Do all of the statements on this list align with the vision of the church? ___yes ___ no (if not, you will need to rework your vision statement until alignment is achieved)
Vision statement draft: *Small groups are Christ-centered, authentic communities where group members experience spiritual growth and care for one another while sharing the love of Christ, serving others, and making a difference in the world.*	Vision statement draft:

Personal Mission Statement Worksheet

Why is a mission statement important to every leader?

It would be a tragedy to get to the end of one's life only to realize important goals had never been achieved and the life lived had not reflected what was valued or considered important. As human beings, we are given a finite amount of time on this earth. Capturing values, purpose, and dreams on paper can be a helpful step toward living a fulfilled life. The process of creating a personal mission statement provides an opportunity to examine your own roles, values, spiritual gifts, talents, and dreams.

A personal mission statement can help you:

◆ Understand what you are supposed to do and why—and what you should not do.
◆ Appreciate the importance of your contributions—to your family, church, and community.
◆ Evaluate opportunities and celebrate successes.
◆ Communicate your life's work to others.
◆ Focus your creativity, efforts, energy, and thinking.

To start, answer these four questions…

◆ *Who am I? (What roles do I have in life? Who has God created me to be?)*
◆ *What do I value? (What do I feel is most important in life?)*
◆ *What do I want to do? (How do I want to invest my time and talents?)*
◆ *What will be my legacy? (At the end of my life, what will I have accomplished?)*

Here is an example:

Who am I?	Parent, wife, child of God
What do I value?	Life-long learning, teaching, serving
What do I want to do?	Invest in people's lives with my time, talents, knowledge, and prayers
What will be my legacy?	God will have used me to equip others to realize their full potential in Christ.

As a wife, mother, and child of god, I will fully use my gifts and passions for learning and serving to invest my time, talents, knowledge, and prayers in the lives of other people, including my family members, so that through my service, God will equip others to realize their full potential in Christ.

Now it's your turn...

Who am I?

_____

What do I value?

_____

What do I want to do?

_____

What will be my legacy?

_____

My personal mission statement...

Creating a Values Statement

SAMPLE

Values of Our Small Group Community:

Open and Honest: Group members are willing to be open and honest within the group, sharing feelings, struggles, and joys while speaking the truth in love to one another.

Sustainable: The measure of authentic small group life is that it is on-going

Growing: Each group member is committed personally to spiritual growth and the group as a whole is growing spiritually, physically, and emotionally.

Affirming: Group members affirm and encourage one another, building each other up in Christ.

Available: Group members make a commitment to the community to not only share their time with one another and to the group process but also their talents, treasure and wisdom in order to meet needs and serve one another.

Safe and Confidential: Being open and honest is built on a commitment that what is said in the group will remain confidential, opinions will be respected, and differences allowed.

Accountable: As relationships deepen and trust develops, members of the group will extend support and help in areas of personal commitments made.

Outwardly focused: Group members serve within the context of the group and outside of the group in Christ's name and are willing to consider using the 'open chair' as a tool for inviting new members to the group.

Biblically Based: Curriculum studies and purpose for small groups are firmly rooted in the understanding of God's Word.

Fun: Groups are intentional in their efforts to make involvement in small group life a joyful experience!

Ministry Values Statement Worksheet

Values of Our _____ Ministry:

_____: _____

_____: _____

_____: _____

_____: _____

_____: _____

_____: _____

_____: _____

_____: _____

_____: _____

_____: _____

Strategic Planning Templates

Reference #	Strategies — Do What?
1.1	
1.2	
1.3	
1.4	

Action Plan

Key Strategy #1

Action Steps		Resource Requirements				
Reference #	Description	Person Responsible	Completion Date	Staff	Budget	Measurable Results
1.1.1						
1.1.2						
1.1.3						
1.1 4						

Action Plan

Key Strategy #2

Action Steps			Resource Requirements			
Reference #	Description	Person Responsible	Completion Date	Staff	Budget	Measurable Results
1.2.1						
1.2.2						
1.2.3						
1.2 4						

Strategic Planning Update Form

Ministry Team _____

Director _____

Significant Accomplishments

    1.

    2.

    3.

Top Opportunity Areas

    1.

    2.

    3.

Key Learnings…

-
-

Next Steps…

-
-

Communicating to Inspire

A Worksheet for Creating an Inspirational Message

Follow this outline, using the tips from Chapter 7, to prepare and draft your inspirational message. Make notes to yourself about how you'll utilize each element.

I. *"Be animated. Use passion, emotion, and activity to help convey the message and create excitement."* What "emotion" words will you use? For example, in one of Martin Luther King, Jr.'s famous speeches, he said, "I have a dream." How will you use activity and body language to get your point across?

II. *"Use vivid language—stories, metaphors, images, and the senses—to make your message come to life."* Think about Ronald Reagan's speech in which he said, "Mr. Gorbachev, tear down that wall!" Or consider Winston Churchill's 1946 speech at Westminster College, during which he used a phrase that came to symbolize the oppression of communism: "From Stettin in the Baltic to Trieste in the Adriatic, an iron curtain has descended across the Continent." What stories, metaphors, images, or senses can you draw upon to capture the essence of your message?

III. *"Use examples the audience can relate to — you want them to be able to see themselves in the story. In a rural community, a farming example makes perfect sense, but this is probably not the best choice for an audience in the urban core."* Who is your audience? What is their frame of reference – their natural environment? What examples from their world can you incorporate into your message?

IV. *"Use repetition. Restate your message in different ways."* Practice phrasing your main point in different ways.

V. *"Be upbeat and positive. Make the goal seem achievable. Your role as leader is to generate hope and aspiration."* What positive language will you use? How can you make the goal appear within reach?

VI. *"Exude personal conviction."* Write here why you believe this goal is worthwhile. Why do you believe it can be attained? If you can articulate that, you are halfway there!

Planning an Interpersonal Conflict Resolution Session

Before the meeting, consider the following questions:

1. What is the desired outcome of this meeting? What is your goal for the relationship/situation, and how would you like to be perceived at the end of the session?

2. What are the potential causes of the conflict? What did each party contribute to the conflict?

3. How do the other people involved perceive the conflict?

4. How might the other people respond to this meeting? How might they feel? What might they say? How could you respond to their feelings/comments?

During the meeting, follow these steps:

1. Establish rapport and ground rules. Set the stage for openness, respect, and mutually satisfactory problem-solving (not criticism).

2. Describe the conflict. Be objective and specific.

3. Ask others to share their perspectives. Listen to what they have to say without assuming you already have all the information you need.

4. Identify the points of agreement and disagreement.

5. Solicit potential solutions from the parties involved. If you are one of the parties, offer your own suggestions.

6. Evaluate the options. Which ones will satisfy all people involved? Remind everyone that the goal is mutual satisfaction, not a victory for one side, and that everyone might have to compromise.

7. Select an option and develop a plan of action. Be specific about who will do what and by when.

8. End the meeting with expressions of appreciation for each person's participation and contribution to the process.

Leading Through Transition

Use this worksheet as a guide as you prepare to lead a group through an upcoming change.

1. Why is the change needed? How will the change make things better? How will you communicate the need for change? What format will you use (e.g., in person, in writing, etc.)?

2. Who are your potential advocates for change? How will you recruit them? What are your expectations of them?

3. What is your vision for the future? Practice communicating the vision in a four- to five-sentence summary that you can repeat/rephrase in various ways. How will you share this vision?

4. How will you authorize team members to plan and implement the change? What boundaries will you give them (i.e., what they can and cannot do without approval)?

5. What are some short-term milestones you can target? What will determine "success"?

6. How will you celebrate success along the way and at the end of the journey?

Ministry Position Description

POSITION TITLE	MINISTRY	DEPARTMENT	RESPONSIBLE TO

RESPONSIBILITIES:

DREAMS FOR:

SPIRITUAL GIFTS:

INDIVIDUALITY:

TALENTS/SKILLS:

EXPERIENCES:

RESOURCES:
Length of Commitment:

MINIMUM SPIRITUAL MATURITY:

Regular Commitments:

ADDITIONAL COMMENTS:

Availability:

Pre-Event Coaching Outline

Use this outline to help your apprentice plan upcoming projects/meetings/ communications.

What is the project? What is the purpose/goal of the project?

What is the timing of the project (date, time, duration, etc.)?

What's your vision for the project? Give a description of the ideal successful event. Why do you think this is the optimal plan? *The goal here is not to question the plan, but to think through all the options.*

Who will you involve?

What role will each person play? What do you expect each person to contribute to the project's success?

What obstacles/hurdles might you have to overcome?

How will you overcome them?

What help do you need from me?

Event Observation Checklist

Use this checklist during an event to help you prepare for your post-event coaching session.

What did you observe that went well? How did the apprentice demonstrate growth in his or her leadership abilities/skills?

How will you acknowledge, affirm and celebrate this fact?

What did you observe that could be improved upon next time?

What skills development or training can you provide to further develop your apprentice's leadership ability for this type of event in the future?

Who, besides the apprentice leader, stretched themselves to greater performance during the event? How will you or your apprentice acknowledge, affirm and celebrate this fact?

Post-Event Coaching Session Outline

Ask your apprentice the following questions. There are no right or wrong answers. Your role is not to provide the answers or to lead your apprentice to any specific answers, but to guide the individual through a process of evaluating the event and his or her performance objectively.

What do you think went well during the planning of the event or the event itself? What skills/abilities do you think you used most effectively? *After the individual responds, make sure to add positive observations you made that he or she missed, and to celebrate those successes.*

Where do you think there is room for improvement? What things didn't go as you had hoped? What would you personally want to do differently next time? *You should have some suggestions prepared in case the individual doesn't have any ideas here. It is most effective if you word these suggestions as collaborative questions instead of directives (i.e., "What do you think about...?").*

What training or resources would help you feel even more equipped for this type of event next time?

Let's develop your plan of action for developing the skills you want to improve upon or attaining the resources needed to achieve greater performance next time. *Include specific action to be taken, date of expected completion, and date for progress reporting/follow-up.*

Who do you need to recognize for their efforts during the event?